Bicycling the Adventure Cycling Northern Tier Trail Across America

Tour Story of Two Sometimes Grumpy Old Men

David E. Siskind

Books About Bicycling
Minneapolis, Minnesota

BICYCLING THE ADVENTURE CYCLING NORTHERN TIER
TRAIL ACROSS AMERICA
Tour Story of Two Sometimes Grumpy Old Men
by David E. Siskind

Published by:
Books About Bicycling
5812 Thomas Circle
Minneapolis, MN 55410-2936
612-929-4498
email: desa@uswest.net

Edited by Marie Barrett
Photographs by Tom O'Brien, Dave Siskind, and Self Timer
Drawings by Theresa Scanlan

First Printing February 2000
Printed in the United States of America

Library of Congress Catalog Card Number: 00-190243
ISBN 0-9678878-0-1 9.95

Acknowledgments

Love for our wives Dana and Lois for their understanding and support during this long time away from home and to our children who refrained from telling us we were crazy to do this.

Thanks to those who read and reviewed this text including biking friends Charles and Renee Weisenberg, my daughter-in-law Michele Milinis, my step-daughter Theresa who provided the sketches, and our professional editor, Marie Barrett.

A good-sport award goes to friend and ex-coworker Tom Smith who rode the first week of challenging terrain in the Washington Cascades and put up with two bike fanatics.

Thanks to those we met on the tour who gave us a slice of the best of America and especially those fellow bicyclists who became, albeit all too briefly, a part of our lives.

Thanks to Stan Rogers and Bill Staines whose songs helped speed the miles.

Finally, eternal friendship and love for Tom O'Brien who was my patient partner for this tour of a lifetime. He was the public relations half of this team always willing and anxious to tell the tales of our adventures. He trusted my navigational instincts which only failed a few times in a thousand decisions. His photos are intermixed with mine and indistinguishable as we sometimes took photos with each others cameras.

Preface

"Are you going to write a book?" The third time somebody asked this, we realized it was because they saw us logging the statistics and notes on this trip as we both do on all our trips. We responded "no" because, by 1998, bicycling coast to coast was no longer a novel feat. Many had done it and many had written about it. In fact, by following an established and mapped-out bike route across America, Adventure Cycling's Northern Tier crossing, we expected to and did meet and ride with many others doing the same big trip.

Even more, we did not expect our "epic" to be a great physical and psychological challenge nor one of personal or philosophical discovery. Many of the great tour stories are triumphs over ignorance, lack of preparation, wrong or bad equipment, mid-life crises, difficult conditions, and/or naivete. While our tour was to be the longest for both of us, we weren't novices and did not expect to find much drama. Yet, it was still a ride of reaffirmation, and a personal "epic." You can't bicycle 5,000 miles and not have *something* happen. We weren't youngsters, and nine weeks on the road inevitably creates some poignant moments, even if only those created by chance, nature, and newly made friends. In summary, we had a great time. This story is worth telling at least for those friends.

Tom, 62, started serious bicycling with the Los Angeles Wheelmen in 1971 and now lives in Portland, Oregon. He had done various tours including one in 1996 from Portland to San Diego. He regularly rides to northern California to visit relatives, has done Cycle Oregon six times, and has taken an organized Adventure Cycling bike-camping tour of the Oregon coast. Interestingly, his many years of cycling had been limited to the three Pacific States. I (David, the narrator) am 56 and started my serious bicycling in 1960 with the Cycling Enthusiasts of Philadelphia. I have bike-toured in most of the States, Canadian Provinces, and countries of Western Europe. I have done a few race miles in the 1960's and more than a few commuting and touring miles, totaling about 350,000.

Chapter 1

Two Rendezvous

Swoosh............Swoosh..............Swoosh.............. What's that noise? I think I know but I'm afraid to look. The Vista bike light showed it was 11:30 p.m. I unzipped the tent door, looked out and saw the industrial-strength lawn sprinkler sweeping and blasting the girls' tent and lightly spraying the others within reach. Harlem, Montana town officials had said the sprinklers *wouldn't come on* because we were camping there. The girls' tent had to be moved and quickly. Scott, their dad, emerged from his tent as did his two very tired, sleepy and wet daughters, Sarah and Lisa, from theirs. We dragged the girls' tent over next to Tom's, my riding partner, who later admitted the commotion awoke him but he was not alert enough to care what was going on. Going back to sleep after the crisis with some worrying thoughts: two sprinklers out of four going. How about the two which weren't? How would I easily move my old Eureka Catskill tent, which is not only full of all my s---, including a propped-up bike, but isn't self standing?

Splat...........Splat..........Oh Great, 1:00 a.m. and it must be the other sprinklers. This time the stream is hitting the rest of the tents including mine. Even more incredibly, we had dragged the girls' tent over on top of one of the now-active sprinkler heads. The tired girls again leave their tent holding their sleeping bags in front of them. Scott and a helper from another tent, Dave DeCamp, also emerged. While someone held on to the sprinkler heads to prevent their turning, others ran around for something, anything, to use. Dave dumped a 55-gallon oil drum being used as a trash can and placed it over the closest sprinkler. That was no good as it boomed like a jet engine in a hollow can. We laughed at this and also wondered how Tom could sleep through all this noise and fuss. We then placed the drum between the sprinkler and the tents, which deflected the water with far less noise. Dave found a second drum for the other sprinkler. At last, back to bed. Tomorrow will be another long biking day. I dropped off to sleep thinking this trip certainly isn't dull, of the start two weeks earlier, and how we got to this point.

2

"Hi Tom." Are we really doing this? Our rendezvous was a third-floor bedroom in the Seattle Youth Hostel, June 11, 1998. Years of fantasizing, a year of planning, and now we're about to embark on the biggest ride we have both ever done: coast-to-coast on Adventure Cycling's Northern Tier route with side trips to the Winnipeg Folk Music festival, my home in Minneapolis, and Iowa's RAGBRAI cross-state ride.

Tom O' Brien and I had met on a three-week tour of Washington State and British Columbia in 1990 organized by mutual friends from the Los Angeles area. Tom knew them from his days living in L.A. and riding with the L.A. Wheelmen. I had met them back in 1972 on one of their bicycling visits to Minnesota. Tom and one of his L.A. friends, Grant, had talked about a cross-the-country tour for many years. By 1997, it appeared Grant wouldn't be able to do the trip and I had told Tom I was interested and wanted to do it soon, like 1998. Both of is felt age creeping up on us. We both also had scheduling problems and obligations requiring setting firm start and end dates. We cleared our respective calendars, decided on a route, each bought a set of Adventure Cycling's maps, and started working on a proposed day-by-day itinerary. We would camp except for a few places having Youth Hostels. The inexpensive nature of Hostels fit our financial plans even if some of them only had dormitory-type accommodations. We decided "no cooking." We would eat out and save both weight and time and we wouldn't make any reservations but wing it every day. This gave us flexibility but anxiety for Tom, as he always meticulously planned and made reservations for his tours. I never did, but then again, I tended to bike-tour in less traveled areas than the Pacific Coast.

Tom had purchased a new Cannondale T 1000 which had the low gears he wanted (down to 19-inches). He equipped it with Bruce Gordon racks, Robert Beckman panniers, a new Terry saddle for men, and a shock- absorbing seat post. He felt it was time to replace his old Nashbar tourer, and he had the money from the loss of his "fast" bike in a bike shop fire in Portland. I had to build a new rear wheel for my well-tested 1974 Holdsworth Cyclone, which had over 70,000 miles on the frame and a fair number on most of the parts as well. My 15 speeds were skewed to the low end (and for techno-readers, all gears were between 27 and 74 inches from most likely the world's only 18-20-23-24-28 freewheel). A commitment, equipment, training, itinerary, and tickets. We were ready.

"You a biker?" asked a man at the SeaTac airport. I was waiting at baggage for my bike and holding my handlebar bag, a dead giveaway. He was there to assist the GTE Big Ride, which involved about 700 fund-raising bikers crossing the USA and starting from Seattle about two days after us. They were taking a more southerly route. We would hear nothing more about them until one complaint in Napoleon, Ohio. "Bikers were everywhere," and a report Tom later got from a GTE ride participant on AMTRAK on his way back to Portland: "Heat, extreme cold, accidents, hit every big city." Sounds like they had *their* drama.

Learning is a lifelong process even for experienced cycle tourists, like not getting lost. I had a map for biking from the airport to downtown Seattle. However, when passing through the parking garage, I must have turned the wrong way and somehow ended up going in the right direction (north, judging from the position of the sun) but on the west side of the airport instead of the intended east side. I wasn't worried as downtown could be seen in the distance and navigation-by-landmarks would get me there, although with more hills and bridges than the "official" route. I blamed Northwest Airlines employees who were having the first of several 1998 labor disputes and caused the plane to leave Minneapolis three hours late. I was groggy and tired even before starting to ride. Confusion continued downtown as I rode around the block three times before figuring out the Youth Hostel was about 50 feet down the hill facing the waterfront. After meeting in the Hostel, Tom and I rode the Seattle waterside bike paths so I could "round out" my day's milage to an even number and we could enjoy exploring the way we like most, from the bike saddle.

Our real journey started the next morning on the 6:20 a.m. ferry to Bainbridge Island on a clear and cool day. I had worried a bit about this 90-mile day northwest to Anacortes knowing the distinct possibility of strong head winds and rain in Puget Sound and the San Juan Islands. We were to rendezvous that night with another rider, also named Tom (Smith from Minneapolis). He was planning to ride the first part of the cross-country ride with us, as far as North Dakota. Port Townsend was our lunch stop and our second ferry ride. Memories of "being there and doing that" surfaced from the 1990 tour when Tom, I, and LA friends moteled in Port Townsend.

"That hammer has to go." "Also half of the big bath towel, extra shoes, heavy jacket..." We had Tom's stuff all over the sidewalk outside of a Mailboxes store in Oak Harbor, half a day out of Seattle. Brutal decisions were being made. It was evident after the first half-day of hills and head winds on Bainbridge and Whidbey Islands that Tom's bike was too heavy for this tour with its expected 80-mile daily distances. Eighteen pounds were shipped home, including both front panniers. Tom later said that there wasn't anything shed that he seriously missed. We continued north after Tom's "sidewalk sale" in Oak Harbor, crossed the always exciting and trafficky bridges at Deception Pass, and rode the many ups and downs of Marine Drive to the Anaco Beach campground outside of Anacortes, Washington. It was, after all, a nice day with weak head winds and no rain.

Tom Smith joined us there, three bikers ready to start the 4,500-mile Adventure Cycling Northern Tier cross-America trail. Smith was an old coworker of mine from the Bureau of Mines. He heard me describing plans to ride across America at one of our reunion luncheons and was interested in doing the first part of the ride. We had gotten in one 95-mile training ride together in the spring, but he had managed relatively few pre-trip miles in contrast to myself with 4,700 and Tom O'Brien with 3,041. He responded to my concerns with: "I may be a little slow but I'll get there." Smith had ridden from Bellingham, Washington after visiting old friends in Vancouver, British Columbia. We set up our tents and dined on the outdoor deck of the very nice Compass Rose restaurant overlooking the San Juan Island ferry dock. Afterwards, I rode alone into Anacortes, both to see the interesting town once again and get an even 100 miles, a "century." That end-day riding would be an almost regular occurrence.

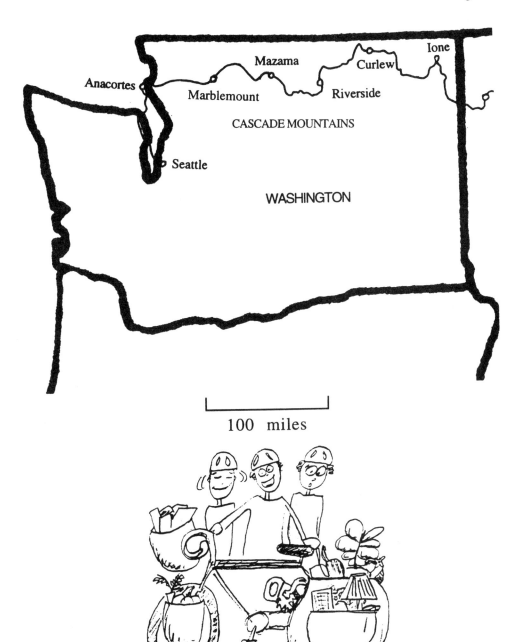

Anacortes
Marblemount
Mazama
Curlew
Ione
Riverside
CASCADE MOUNTAINS
Seattle
WASHINGTON

100 miles

Chapter 2

Warm-Up For The Mountains

"There has got to be a store or restaurant somewhere." Anxious to
hit the road and hoping to catch or meet other bikers at every turn of
the "official trail," we decided to roll off a few miles and then stop
for breakfast. Just after crossing I-5 at 25 miles we found it.
Slightly cranky, I expressed a desire to limit future pre-breakfast
milage to 10. We continued on to Sedro Woolley and Concrete
where Smith decided that it was time for *him* to shed a few pounds
of load. (I thought, am I next?) He waved down the driver of a UPS
truck and had him take about five pounds of his stuff. Even then,
Smith still had lots, including fishing and cooking gear. For him,
this was to be a camping trip with a little biking, while for Tom
O'Brien and myself, camping was the enabler and biking was the
main idea.

I had some concerns as this first day was to be our only warm-up
before serious climbing in the northern Cascades. Riding in
Minnesota is scarce preparation for mountain climbing. If the Toms
had similar concerns, they didn't voice them. We had nice tail winds
and climbed gradually from sea level to about 600 feet elevation at
Marblemount, Washington, our campground for the first night on
the "route." Washington State is beautiful but with some slightly
disturbing aspects. O'Brien said the woods are full of isolationist
militia, the aggressive-seeming pick-up trucks had gun racks and
political bumper stickers, and there were a few "Impeach Clinton"
signs (this was before Ken Starr's report on the President and
Monica). Generally, we avoided political talk.

We did talk biking and biking styles, however. Evident that first day
were our different riding styles. I was used to flat-land cruising at
100 rpm in a 54-inch gear (46-23), corresponding to 15 or 16 mph.
Tom O'Brien had had a serious accident four years earlier that
involved a hip reconstruction. He had no real push on the injured leg
and relied on a very fast cadence. On the flats, he would stay with
me; however, minor hills and head winds slowed him to 11 to 13
mph. To his frustration, he was also slower on the downhills. His

total weight was about the same as mine, so we attributed this to his wind-catching wider panniers and top-rack load. Tom Smith was slower yet, especially on the climbs. His still-heavier load, high gears with low cadence, pedal-and-rest style, and lack of sufficient training miles were discussed. But Smith dismissed them as unimportant and instead blamed heredity - his lack of fast-twitch muscles. This first day was the only day we all three arrived at the destination together.

"We have a problem." O'Brien and I came back from the shower building in Clark's campground in Marblemount to a geyser next to our tents. Apparently Smith had bumped and broken off a plastic RV hook-up water pipe while hanging up some clothes to dry. Tom said he barely touched it. We all stood around watching the new lake spread towards our tents while youths working for the owner tried to stem the flow or find the shutoff. Trying to "cap" it sent the flow tens of feet high. I was thinking "we're toast." At the least, we'll have to move our tents. At the worst, they will throw us out. Tom O'Brien had negotiated a good price for camping with our three small tents on one RV site, and the woman in charge wasn't sure the absent owner would later approve of the deal. We were very careful the rest of our stay, ate in their restaurant, and fed the resident campground bunnies. Nobody said anything to us about our camp fee or water incident and hopefully bikers are still welcome there.

Chapter 3

Cascade Mountains of Northern Washington

"Lets leave him a sandwich." O'Brien and I were on a break near the twin summits of Rainy Pass (4,855 feet) and Washington Pass (5,477 feet) on U.S. Highway 20 in north-central Washington State. Knowing we would encounter no stores or restaurants for many miles and hours, we carried a jar of peanut butter, saved from the pile of O'Brien's homeward-bound stuff in Oak Harbor, and also a loaf of bread. Smith was an hour or two behind, so we rubber banded a sandwich to a roadside reflector post in a bag with his name on it and hoped he would notice it. I had also picked up a new-looking Bike Friday water bottle someone had left on a guardrail post. I have a Bike Friday at home (a folding bike from Green Gear in Eugene, Oregon) and thought I would keep it as an extra bottle for those long climbs. Also, we had been hearing about "three guys and a girl" somewhere ahead of us and thought the bottle might belong to one of them.

The climbs were warm but the fast descents cold and windy. Gusty winds around every bend made my bike shudder and speeds over 35 sometimes felt scary. Tom's bike seemed less affected. Our destination was Mazama, Washington, which turned out to have a nice outing supply store and a grocery. "Real food" was only to be found at the Mazama Inn where O'Brien and I feasted on huge platters of ribs and wondered how long it would be until Smith pulled in. After dinner, we biked five miles more to Rocking Horse campground. O'Brien talked them into letting us "camp" in their old office building saving us from having to put up tents. The day's distance of 83 was a long way from 100. However, I rode back towards Smith and found him just as he was pulling into Mazama about two hours behind us. He thanked me for the sandwich. I told him about the Inn and campground and went off to clock my century. O'Brien noted how nice people could be, from his talking with the young lady running the Mazama store (an escapee from big-city life), the grocery people who stayed open late for us and specially for Smith, and the campground people who trusted the honesty of strangers.

The next day was breakfast in the wild-west-looking town of Winthrop, Washington and a warm-up ride to strangely -named Twisp in preparation for the 2,500-foot climb to Loup Loup Pass (4,020 feet). I established a then-record speed for this tour of 46.5 mph on the fast and exciting descent to Okanogan. O'Brien and I waited for Smith for over an hour and then decided to press on to Riverside under worsening skies. Waiting and debating in Riverside were renewed when a tired Smith arrived. There was uncertainty about the rain holding off and how hard it would be to press on to Tonasket against a strong quartering wind. I was concerned about losing ground so early in the trip. However, by consensus we called it a day. The campground was pleasant but dinner was sparse in this small town's bar.

The following morning had the same northwest wind but at least no rain threat. In Tonasket, conversations among the locals in our breakfast restaurant were on the closed roads to and around Republic and over Sherman Pass. Apparently, heavy rains and widespread washouts had closed mountain roads, some for all summer. Tom Smith appeared to get the definitive advice. It involved riding U.S. 20 to Wauconda where we could pick up a side road detour north to Curlew, which reportedly had a campground. Then, we would continue east, doing Boulder Pass rather than the tougher Sherman, and come back south along the Kettle and Columbia Rivers. That is what O'Brien and I did. Near Wauconda and the summit, we caught up with Dick and Marilyn Clothier, a tandeming couple from Sacramento also going coast to coast. They were pulling a Bob trailer and moving rather slowly, having trouble with their trailer's tire, which was disintegrating.

After lunch in Wauconda, O'Brien and I enjoyed a beautiful run down through the forest and along the Kettle River to Curlew. We found the campground, set up tents, and I went out to add to my day's total of 77 miles. Within 1/2 mile of the campground, I came upon Dick and Marilyn heading out of town after a local cop cruising in his car told them there was no camping in town. After pointing the way to the campground, I continued south towards Republic to see how far I could get. I soon found Smith who apparently didn't come the way we had and the way he himself determined was the best in that morning's Tonasket restaurant conversations. Apparently, at Wauconda, he saw the slight rise of the road (100 yards prior to the 30-mile descent) we had taken and decided it looked too hard. He had missed a great all downhill ride through the woods with almost no traffic.

In Curlew, we watched the late afternoon buildup of clouds and scattered showers like we had the previous day. This pattern would continue most days throughout the West as far as eastern North Dakota. We regularly ducked under cover and waited it out. This strategy worked well until a northern Minnesota all-day storm nailed us good. We felt lucky to have escaped Puget Sound dry but were surprised to see regular rain in the eastern Washington semi-desert and also in the long prairie lands of Montana and Dakota. In our planning and thinking, we expected and feared these long reaches across the prairie would have wilting sun and possibly fierce winds. Fortunately, it wasn't to be.

I had my only spill in Curlew: on a sandy patch in an unpaved driveway doing about two mph. It was an easy flop to the side with no damage to rig or self other than some superficial bleeding and some imbedded gravel particles. Tom O'Brien had already had his only spill on the bridge at the north end of Bainbridge Island our first day when he also did an easy side flop when his front panniers hit the curb while negotiating an expansion strip. He wasn't hurt either.

Leaving Curlew, O'Brien and I lost Smith on the Boulder Pass climb and rode to and down the rivers to rejoin the "official route" on the eastern side of the closed stretch of U.S. 20. We started to park our bikes at a restaurant. But then, thinking about how long we might have to wait, we decided we would roll on at an easy pace rather than stiffening up in an hour or more of sitting around. Through Kettle Falls and Coleville, we started to climb a grade that felt harder than the map profile suggested. A quick and hard shower caught us and we waited it out under the porch roof of a trailer which had nobody around. Despite having rain gear, stuff packed in plastic, and fenders on the bikes, riding in the rain gets the bike, riders and gear wet, dirty, and gritty. We tried to avoid this by seeking cover even if it was only under broadleaf trees. All day we saw UPS trucks and thought "Here come tires for Dick and Marilyn's trailer." We had left them temporarily stuck in Curlew.

We finally pulled into the proposed overnight, Beaver campground and resort on Little Pend Oreille Lake. I was ready to celebrate: we pulled this off and we didn't even get wetter than a few drops. A note awaited us there: "Tom (Smith) is staying on in Kettle Falls. Will continue at a slower pace. He will then take the train (to Minnesota) from Spokane. He wishes you good and thanks for everything." We were down to two sooner than expected. We didn't blame him as he wasn't likely enjoying the ride and especially the climbs. While I was getting ready to check in, O'Brien said "lets go for the town of Ione." This would make up the half day we lost earlier and get us back on schedule. Problem was that the steep road down off the mountain was under repair, wet, and muddy from the previous rain which could (and did) start again. It wasn't the most enjoyable of downhills but we did it. Rather than setting up tents in the rain, we made it our first motel overnight and quit that day at 94 miles. This was one of those days earning the "high five."

We entered Idaho from Washington State by riding along the Pend Oreille River with a lunch stop in Usk. Continuing east, we could see rain showers over our right shoulders. Tom Smith would later tell us he was riding in those showers. We rode around Newport looking for a "Welcome to Idaho" sign to photograph. Returning to the route, we followed wooded and mountain-lined valleys on a beautifully clear and cool day to an RV campground on U.S. 95 outside of Sandpoint, Idaho. We picked a spot as far from the highway as possible to get some quiet. Tom said he heard trains all night. This would turn out to be an omen for the ride across Montana.

The bike path into Sandpoint used an old highway bridge across scenic Lake Pend Oreille, and then the route continued along the lake towards Montana. Low threatening clouds were disquieting, but good tail winds lightened the riding. After lunch in a bar-restaurant complete with a pet pig, showers finally caught us in the Bull River Valley. We spent short periods hiding in the trees and then a long period in a cowboy bar. Tom later liked to tell how all heads turned and stared when we entered the bar in our riding lycra-spandex but nobody bothered us as we sipped our soft drinks next to the window and waited out the rain. After a while, we waited outside on their covered porch and counted pickup trucks. When the rain stopped, we made a successful dash for Troy, Montana, where we found the RV campground and a restaurant only 1/2-hour from closing. Riding around later to add to the day's 93 miles, I encountered the first "Male Youths in Cars" who seemed threatening. Did my first laundry using the campground's washer and drier. Tom and I handled this mundane task differently. I had six changes with me and did a full laundry weekly. Tom had basically two outfits, a red one and a blue one, and he washed clothes every day.

Tom's left hip had started acting up this day, the one he had surgery on four years ago. He could ride but was concerned about what to do if it worsened. I worried too. Climbing up to explore some rock caves along the highway probably hadn't helped. Fortunately, the hip was better the next day.

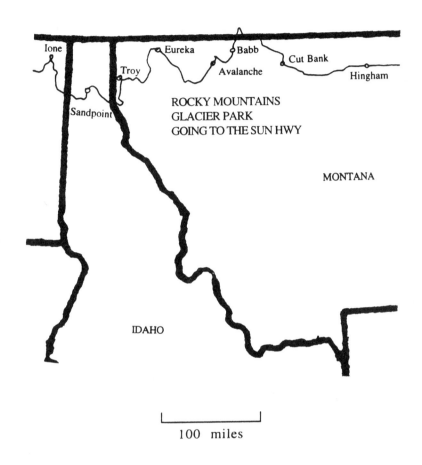

Ione

Eureka

Babb

Cut Bank

Troy

Avalanche

Hingham

Sandpoint

ROCKY MOUNTAINS
GLACIER PARK
GOING TO THE SUN HWY

MONTANA

IDAHO

100 miles

Chapter 4

Rockies

"They are 10 minutes ahead of you," responded the rock climbers to my question "Have you seen any other bikers?" I spun up the revolutions to catch them. This was the end of a nice day's ride on a scenic hilly road past Libby Dam and along Lake Koocanusa where, until then, Tom and I had pretty much stayed together. I quickly caught up with two guys and a girl from East Lansing, Michigan. One was riding a Bike Friday. I asked them what happened to the other guy and they said there wasn't "another guy." Is this the "three guys and a girl" we heard about a week ago or is that another group somewhere still ahead? We never did find out. The next thing I asked was if one had lost a water bottle, which I knew was in plain view under a bungee on top of my stuff. The Friday rider had and was astounded that it had caught up to him. I surrendered the well-traveled prize. With Ken and Gary was Karen. She reminded me of a special female biker friend I had a few lifetimes back. I fell in love in only the way you can for someone you will likely never see again except in a picture (actually, I took three). I did remind Tom that perhaps we will catch this group in New York or so, but we never did. Even while a little jealous of Ken and Gary, I hoped they had a good tour.

After Tom caught up, we conversed a while and then reluctantly left them to their camping in Rexford. We continued on to Eureka, Montana to shorten our next day's approach to Glacier Park. Eureka was in the shadow of the Rockies and suggested excitement to come and work too. It was a noisy town with a continual parade of fast and loud cars driven by the all too common and aggressive young-male-drivers.

Father's Day. I hung around after breakfast to phone my kids while Tom went ahead. US 93 to Whitefish was busy, narrow, and headwindy. After not being able to reach anybody and leaving five messages for kids and stepkids, I chased along after Tom who was anything but slow this day. After a good hour of riding, I spotted him waving from the side of the road with four other bikers. Tom had just met Scott and Ann Weigle and their daughters Sarah, age 15 and Lisa, age 13. Scott and the girls were crossing the country and would be mostly using the Adventure Cycling Northern Tier route. Ann could only ride for one week and was to AMTRAK home to Seattle from Whitefish. We talked and took pictures and then our leave, not expecting to see them again. But we would, luckily.

After lunch in Whitefish, we made our worst highway choice until much later in Boston, Massachusetts. The Adventure Cycling map showed two options for the approach to West Glacier, one paved all the way (U.S. 2) and one with 5 miles of gravel. We choose the paved one and were lucky to have survived the trucks, RV's, and trailers on the narrow, curvy and very fast road on a Sunday afternoon. Later, on the AMTRAK back to Portland, Tom was told by other bicyclists that the gravel stretch wasn't bad. We wished the map had given us more definitive advice at this point. On the good side, Tom had found a dollar bill alongside the road. Tom was always looking for coins on the road and on town streets and always finding some. Tom advises future riders to take the gravel, as the scary road wasn't worth the dollar. We were welcomed into Glacier Park by a nice doe-eyed ranger named Christine and proceeded to McDonald Lodge for a great dinner. After dinner, we rode seven miles to Avalanche Creek campground. Our strategy here was based on the Park's prohibition of bikes on Logan Pass's Going-To-The-Sun-Highway between 11 a.m. and 4 p.m. because of the narrowness and heavy rubber-necking traffic. We wanted to be as close as possible to the climb the next morning so as to ensure we would summit before 11.

Glacier National Park near and east of Avalanche Creek is awesome with snow-tipped mountains towering close and high like I had seen on my six bike tour visits to Banff and Jasper Parks in Canada. I was too energized to sit around camp and rode off to explore the gentle lower part of the climb towards Logan Pass' garden wall lit by the setting sun. Met a couple parked alongside the road watching grizzley bears in the high meadows with binoculars. I arrived back at camp just at dark with a day total of 112 miles. There I found Tom talking with other bike tourists in the section of the campground where the ranger concentrates the bikers. Dave DeCamp and Julia are teachers from San Francisco riding to Vermont to get married. A Hawaiian was rocketing his way to New Jersey, and one strangely decorated bike and tent went unspoken for. We would meet this equipment owner later. There was no hot water in the campground and our first night without showers. This was also our coolest night and we slept thinking about bears.

The climb up the garden wall of Logan Pass was a trip highlight. We twiddled up in our lowest gears for three hours. I used about two dozen opportunities to photograph Tom and the scenery as we climbed high above the valley and past the snow piles which had closed the road only a few days earlier. Summating at 10:15, we found the Hawaiian who had left before us and a cranky ranger who wanted us to park our bikes too far from where we could watch them. We snacked in the parking lot and then proceeded down the less spectacular eastern slope. After lunch in St. Mary, we rode to Babb, Montana (Leaning Tree campground and restaurant on the Black Feet Reservation) and made it a short day, catching up on postcards to friends in the shadows of the tall peaks. Tom had the largest and best hamburger steak of his life by which he was to thereafter compare others.

"Whose route?" "Adventure Cycling, that is who." We got some advice about a good shortcut near Cardston, Canada and its use depended whether it was worthwhile going by way of the Chief Mountain International Highway. Instead of giving a simple answer, this particular local expert was telling us our whole route was wrong and proceeded to redesign how to bike across Montana. We gave up on him and committed ourselves to the shortcut. It took us north into Canada and on to Port of Del Bonita, with tail winds, on a good road, and with essentially no traffic: cycling paradise. Back on the official route, we returned to the States via a bored border post customs official who must see many bikers. All day I was pedalling ahead of Tom, stopping, and taking his photo and the Glacier Park mountains behind him as they receded into the distance. We camped in a windy draw in Cut Bank, Montana on the edge of the prairie and enjoyed our last views of serious mountains until the Alleghenys.

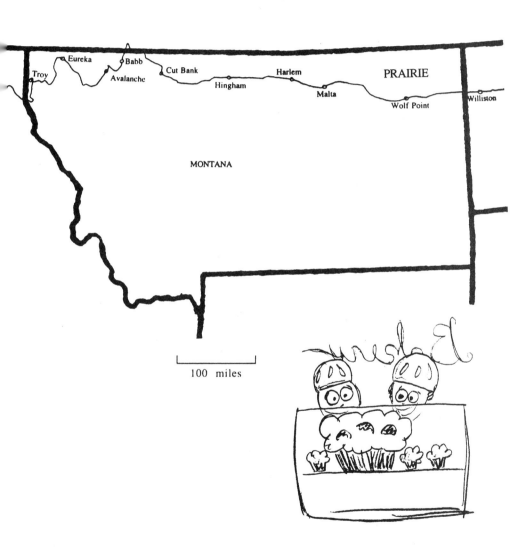

Troy
Eureka
Babb
Avalanche
Cut Bank
Hingham
Harlem
Malta
PRAIRIE
Wolf Point
Williston

MONTANA

100 miles

Chapter 5

The Western Prairie

Tired. Didn't sleep well as the gale winds whipping up the draw flapped my tent fly all night even though I had shortened and tightened my tie lines several times. Tom's new REI Half Dome didn't have this problem. Fortunately, we had wonderful tail winds and cruised easily through Big Sky County to Shelby, Chester, and some highway seal-coating-in-process to Hingham, Montana. This town was about four blocks square, but none of the streets were paved. Looking strange to me, a city person, home driveways were paved down to the dirt street. We camped on a nice grassy park in the middle of this small town. Scott and his daughters showed up and then Dave DeCamp and Julia. Scott and girls had taken U.S. 2 around the south end of Glacier Park, which was both shorter and easier than Logan Pass. We had also apparently underestimated their riding strength.

Tom and I left at 7:00 am the next day as the others slept on. Did about 10 miles before breakfast, and continued on U.S. 2 through Havre, which was too busy and noisy for our tastes. The Montana prairie was prettier and more interesting than we expected. It was green rather than the expected brown or yellow, and we watched distant small mountains slowly fall behind as we traveled. Tom was excited to watch the cattle run alongside us inside their fences in the gently rolling terrain. Temperatures were moderate instead of the heat we had expected and feared. Tail winds also added to the general enjoyment. In places, the road shoulder was small or non-existent, but traffic was generally light. Most motorists must have been on the interstate, and bikes on U.S. 2 were probably a common sight. Pulled into Harlem and set up our tents in the park next to the swimming pool after Tom cleared it with city officials. Tom noted the sign on a box in the park with the sprinkler watering schedule. He asked a town official about it and was told that (someone) comes at 2:00 a.m. and, if there are campers, he doesn't turn on the sprinklers. Ha!!!

Scott and the girls arrived later, as did Dave and Julia. Even though the sky was doing its usual afternoon thickening, the other bikers broke Tom and Dave's #1 rule of bike camping: set up the tents first. They parked their bikes and went swimming in the pool on this hot afternoon. Soon, Tom and I were diving for our tents as the shower hit and listening to the others scrambling to set up tents and get their gear inside. Later that night there would be a lot more scrambling when the sprinklers started. The next morning, Tom again saw the town official he had spoken to as he walked by on his way to work, but he wouldn't look at us.

"It is starting to rain. Let's wait a little while and see what it does." Tom and I had gotten off to a fast start (50 miles in 3 hours and 20 minutes) and just finished lunch in Malta, Montana. We were about to continue on. Watching the rain get heavier and an east (head) wind come up, we sheltered in a store being used for construction storage, restless but dry and comfortable, and watched the road and the rain. When Scott and girls splashed by, I ran out to speak to them. They had rain gear on and were going to try to keep moving. After a few hours, Tom and I gave up and scouted for a cheap motel room. The next day, we were still waiting and it was the same room for a second night. I read most of the book I had along. To avoid going cabin-crazy, we went to the town's only movie theater that night and watched Godzilla with about 20 other kids.

"It's not raining. Lets hit the road!" Before leaving Malta, we found that Dave and Julia had also holed up in Malta, but in a different motel and apparently hitting different restaurants. We were warned about mosquitos in Seco and found them. Driven by strong tail winds, "It doesn't get any better than this," we were in Glasgow by lunch (70 miles by 12:10). After lunch, Tom got a head start as I stopped to retie my shoe laces. Even though he had only a minute or so on me, I couldn't catch him until I reached and held a sustained pace of 25 mph in my highest (although not very high) gear. Just as I closed to 20 feet or so he stopped to write in his ever-present notebook: "100 miles in 5 hours and 49 minutes, a new personal record." Tom had been pushing his 103-inch gear. We pulled into Wolf Point with 124 miles on the clock, having made up one day of the time we had lost in Malta. Another High Five.

We hadn't found Scott and his daughters, but there was a biker in the motel lawn campground and we stopped to talk. He greeted us with "you must be Tom and Dave" and we responded with "Oh, you're the bike." He was a stranger to us but his bike wasn't. Tom recognized it as the bike from Avalanche Creek Campground in Glacier Park. That's how we met Jason Snell, a biker from Michigan who had ridden all over the mountainous west before hitting the trail east we were now on. At the Avalanche creek campground, he was hiking with some girls he had met when we were setting up our tents. He was still sleeping when we left early the next morning. Later, Dave and Julia arrived as did another biker, Mike. We almost had a party that night although wondering, where are Scott and the girls?

Tom and I realized, by this time, that following an established long-distance route would mean that we would have other bikers for company. We were constantly being told that bikers were x days or hours ahead. It seemed that all the bikers knew who was ahead of them and sometimes also behind and who was passing in the other direction. We tended to stop at the same convenience stores and select the same restaurants. There is a bicycle fellowship which surfaces on epic trips. I knew this from a similar experience in Yugoslavia in 1979 and was told the same by a Minneapolis friend, Mike Reudy, who rode the length of North and South America about 20 years ago.

We departed Montana and entered North Dakota near Williston. The road was surprisingly hilly and the surface less than ideal. At least, we thought, we were done with the unlimited speed limit of Montana and the many roadside crosses they used to mark road fatalities Thickening clouds chased us to Williston, and Tom and I couldn't keep up with a much younger (26) and stronger Jason. We camped in the city park (Davidson) and showered in a nearby recreation building, both for free. We also discovered the bounty of the Bonanza Steak House, with it's endless salad bar. I rode around and checked out the other city parks in a futile search for Scott and the girls (and to get my 100). We had been told they were ahead of us and were hoping they would stop in Williston. Met a local biker, Aaron, who also rode along with us out of town the next morning, and said he wished he could go all the way. He had done a long bike tour a few years back but is now tied to home and work.

The official route left U.S. 2 for North Dakota Highway 1804, named for part of the Lewis and Clark expedition. Climbing and

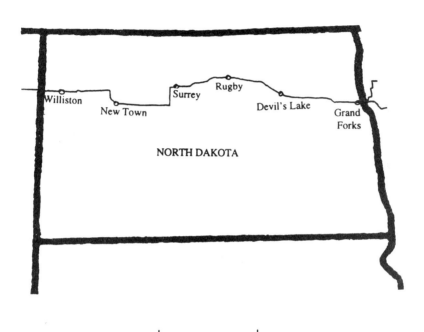

100 miles

descending long hills in the grasslands north of Lake Sakakawea (dammed up Missouri River), we met an older biker (age is relative) on a recumbent who was heading west. He had left the East Coast May 28th (33 days earlier). He looked very capable and comfortable and also told us that he had just passed Scott and the girls and they were not far ahead. They had bypassed Williston where we had overnighted. Tom told me to go for it but I had no ambition to sprint for a half hour and thought we would eventually catch them at our cruising pace.

"There they are." Tom spotted them about two miles ahead on the uphill side of the valley facing us. When we caught them it was reunion time and we rode and talked about all our respective adventures since Malta, Montana. They rode in the rain we had sat out. Riding together, we kept a wary eye on lightning and heavy rain to our rear and also enjoyed the occasional vistas of the lake as we rode into New Town, North Dakota.

The Adventure Cycling map said to check in with the Police. They let us camp behind the station and use the shower facilities inside. We got the feeling there were safety issues in New Town, although the only disquiet we experienced were constant firecrackers (July 4th was approaching). Jason showed up, wet from the storms we saw behind us, and we all had an exciting evening doing laundry. In New Town we had our only mischief, a prank. The local kids put a stray kitten in Tom's tent which was frightened and made a mess inside. This was the only instance on the trip of someone going into one of our tents.

The ride to Minot was warm but uneventful for the six of us. Picnicked in a grassy area between the lanes of Highway 83 south of Minot and then rode uphill into town. There, I bought a new water bottle as my old one was turning into a terrarium. The city was very busy and we decided to roll on a little farther to the small town of Surry. There was no one to ask about our camping in the town park, and a nearby resident saw us setting up and called the police. One came and we talked. No problem except he wanted to be sure we'd be moving on in the morning. We wondered if he even would have let us stay that night if we hadn't had the girls with us. Apparently, most bikers on the route stopped in Minot. It seemed that few people knew that a national cross-country bike route passed through their area, but many noticed that passing loaded-up bikers were a regular thing. With no restaurant in town, we had pizza in the mini-mart. With no hot water in the park, this was our second night (out of 20 so far) without showers. Perhaps Minot would not have been such a bad idea after all.

I called Tom Smith at his home from Minot. This is where he originally was to leave us and this was the date (July 1). He described his riding to Spokane, rain near Usk, Washington, and said he saw us from the window as he AMTRAKed across Montana. He also had no hard feelings about the whole experience.

Scott and his daughters, Jason, Tom, and I traveled together from New Town, North Dakota to Minnesota. Everyone seemed to enjoy riding with constant conversation, stories, jokes, and even singing. The girls were very strong, which was fortunate as they cruised in their highest gears. I told them the advantages of lower gears and spinning more but they were happy with the way they had been riding. They were managing well even on the long tough days. Scott would sometimes get ahead of them and then wait for them to catch up. I was taking so many photos that they named me "Captain Camera." Scott is a Doctor and a bike commuter back home. Jason is big, young, and strong and the fastest despite an enormous load which always included food. He works in a bike shop. The girls are of course still in school.

Threatening skies chased us through Granville (temporarily changed to McGillicuddy for a liquor company contest) and on to Rugby, the geographic center of North America. After showering at the pool, we sheltered from the rain in the Dairy Queen with Dave, Julia, and Mike who had caught up with us. We were there so long that Tom was going to ask for a job. We also pondered the high cost of camping in Rugby during the Pierce County Fair and where the campground charged by-the-tent and not site. Someone told us about the space behind the Eagle Auxiliary Service Club, where we were able to camp for free. Went to the Fair that night but missed seeing Daryl's Racing Pigs.

Our tail winds failed us the next day as we trudged 61 miles (seemed like more) under low clouds to Devils Lake, North Dakota. We had to negotiate our way into the State Park as many of the sites were underwater from the rising lake level. The next day was clear but still with the easterly head winds. I gave my usual advice for head winds, the four downs: slow down, gear down, drop down (on the drops) and calm down (go smoothly). In reality, the head winds we did encounter were not very stiff and that would be generally true throughout the West-to-East cross-country trip. We rode to Lakota for breakfast. For some reason, we kept forgetting this name. We ended up calling it, and any other towns whose names escaped us, "Yocum."

The Red River of the North and Minnesota were within reach. Despite the head winds, the group, and especially our girls, decided a worthwhile goal for this day was Grand Forks, North Dakota, where July 4th fireworks were expected. It was one of those "we pulled this off" epics of 105 miles into the wind. Abandoned the idea of camping when the campground manager insisted on $18.50 per tent ($95 for five tents) for a semi-grassy area that wasn't even nice. Found a motel (Happy Host) and got two nice rooms for the six of us for $79 total, including breakfast coffee and donuts.

We all biked downtown for the celebrations and fireworks that evening. Ate at the food booths, rode over and back across the Red River bridges to Minnesota, and looked at the destruction from the 1997 floods. At dusk, Tom and I picked a spot on the grass and in the crowd and waited for the fireworks. I took a quick spin around the area to see if I could find Scott, the girls, and Jason. When I returned and sat down next to Tom, a little boy of about three came over to us with a blanket and said "for the bikers." I looked around and saw people about 25 feet away looking, smiling, and nodding at us. I jokingly asked Tom if he had told everyone within hearing distance about our trip. He had. We found the others after the fireworks and rode back to the hotel afterwards in the dark using Tom's and my lights. Later that night it rained very hard and we were doubly glad we hadn't camped.

Winnipeg, Manitoba

Birds Hill, Manitoba

St. Malo, Manitoba

Lake Bronson

Warren

Grand
Forks

Oklee

Itasca Park

Breezy Point

Mora

MINNESOTA

Minneapolis

Waterville

Clear Lake

Cedar Falls

Eldora

Monticello

Clinton

IOWA

100 miles

Chapter 6

Minnesota and the Big Detour North

Grand Forks is where Tom and I had planned to turn north and ride to Winnipeg, Canada, for their Folk Music Festival. This was a given for us from the start although Tom didn't know exactly what the festival was about. This hard-to-explain annual event is attended by 15,000 to 20,000 fans and has about 100 musical performers from around the world, but mostly the USA and Canada. I had been talking it up to the group. Jason, Scott, and his daughters liked the idea of the festival and decided to detour there with us, pick up tickets at the gate, attend the festival, and then continue their ride east. I liked that idea too as I really wanted to delay losing our new friends. I also wanted them to meet my family who were driving up to the festival. Unfortunately, this detour took us away from the others, Dave, Julia, and Mike, whom we assume proceeded east.

Minnesota is my home State and I hoped for a nice impression. Unfortunately, what we got was rain storms and the worst mosquitos of the trip, with nowhere else even coming a close second. The rain of early morning resumed after we had departed Grand Forks, and my attempts to shelter from it separated me from the group. Jason was also behind from waiting in Grand Forks for the bike shop to open. Each of our small groups separately plowed into wind and cold driving rain to Warren, Minnesota ("it doesn't get any worse"). This was Tom's and my first real soaking of the trip. The only other was the last day's ride into Boston. Jason caught up to me and we found the others in Warren, waiting under an overhang. They had already located the local motel and we all decided we had had enough of this after only 37 miles. Jason was concerned about the costs and went to a nearby and very wet campground. We spread out our wet stuff, turned up the heat and went for dinner and also to the Dairy Queen. As with the previous night, we went to bed worrying about the next day's weather.

Better: some tail winds and no rain. We had an easy schedule as the distance to the festival site northeast of Winnipeg was 2-1/2 riding days from Grand Forks and we had five days to do it. After 58 miles, we camped at Lake Bronson State Park on the lake and enjoyed a cool and breezy evening with s'mores around the campfire after cleaning up and oiling the bikes. I showed the girls how oiling the chain and derailleur idler wheels noticeably reduces the crank's turning force. The mosquitos arrived that night, as those who have nocturnal out-of-tent events discovered. Several of us spent most of the night swatting the pests and staining the tent walls with our own blood.

The next day we did a fast break-camp and hit the road to Canada. After the tiny town of Tolstoy, with its Eastern Orthodox church, we pulled into beautiful St. Malo Provincial Park. There were far fewer blood-suckers there. The next day's short but trafficky ride took us to a campground just south of Winnipeg where we could ride into the city for an urban tourist holiday. Cycling was a bit harrowing in the Winnipeg area, as few roads have paved shoulders. At least there were no navigational problems, as I have ridden this way nine previous times to earlier music festivals.

After setting up camp, all six of us rode into town to visit local sites including Broadway and the Forks area of the revitalized riverfront. We made an exciting dash through traffic to find the Home Made Music store for festival tickets and then to Chinatown, which was modest compared to New York, San Francisco, etc. The next day was a short ride to Birds Hill Park where we set up camp, went riding on the park bike paths, swam at the beach, bumped into an old family friend, and went back to camp to await my family who were driving up from Minneapolis. When wife Dana, her two daughters Theresa and Elizabeth, and Elizabeth's friend Sarah arrived (now have two "Sarahs"), we helped them set up their tents and make dinner. We then all drove the two miles to the festival site for the first night's concerts. Other friends arrived later, including the "Arrowheads" Bike Team, named not after the arrowhead shape of northern Minnesota but because they wear arrows on their helmets when they ride RAGBRAIs in Iowa (as if they had been shot by Native Americans of old).

For the next three days and nights it was a lot of music with a little morning biking around the park, plus the traditional 30-mile ride to the nearby town of Selkirk, Manitoba for breakfast. During the day there were six performance stages going with different groups every 1/2 to 1 hour on each. In the evening, we sat on our tarps and beach chairs at the "Main Stage" with six to eight acts scheduled to about 1 a.m. Although the performers and the whole scene were new to him, Tom enjoyed the festival and most liked The Arrogant Worms, Trout Fishing in America, and Heather Bishop. Heather had spoken about accompanying a friend on a long bike trip in one of her day acts. Tom went behind stage and told Heather about our ride to Winnipeg from Seattle. That evening on the main stage in front of perhaps 20,000 people, she announced about our whole group (of six) riding across the country and stopping at the festival and then performed a song with the theme "you're never too old."

The Festival was over all too soon and it was time to break up the party and the riding team. Scott, his girls, and Jason were going to head east along the northern edge of Minnesota to Wisconsin, Upper Michigan, and points east. Tom and I were to go south, through Minneapolis, and on to Iowa for our second special event, the second half of Iowa's RAGBRAI ride. We wouldn't see the others again although we wrote postcards to their home addresses. I kept in touch with Dana, and Scott called her to see if a New England hookup with Tom and I was possible. It turned out not to be, although we tried.

Enroute to Minneapolis, Dana gave Tom and me a lift back to Grand Forks, North Dakota. This saved us two riding days so we could resume our west-to-east trip without a geographic break and give us the time in Minneapolis to service the bikes. Unfortunately, all the packing, breakfast, loading, and driving meant we didn't start to pedal until 2:30 p.m. We had to cover 73 miles to a friend's house before dark in 90+ degree heat that seemed hotter with the tail winds. We made it, though barely. I had a flat on that ride, my first puncture and second tire "problem" of the trip (Tom had no flats in the entire 5,500 miles). Our destination was Harold and Shirley Cyr's in Oklee, Minnesota whom I had met nine years earlier while sheltering from a storm on my second annual ride from Minneapolis to Winnipeg. They temporarily suppressed their desire to talk while we cleaned up and Shirley found some food which seemed like ambrosia to two tired and hungry bikers. *Then* we talked.

We only made a few miles the next day before the threatening-looking skies opened up as we sprinted for shelter under trees on a farmhouse lawn. Tom spoke to the lady of the house, who invited us in for better shelter and cookies. That is how we met Dale and

Bonnie Cotes. It turned out that I knew Bonnie's sister Mary, who had been married to a biker in the Minneapolis area (Jim Jahoda). They also knew Harold and Shirley, which was not surprising as we were still close to Oklee and the Cyrs ran the Oklee hardware store for many years.

We continued on to the town of Trail, another wait for rain, and then to Shevlin. This is a tiny town on good old U.S. Highway 2, the road ridden so many miles earlier in Montana. We snacked there, but our day's destination was 22 more miles south to the Youth Hostel in Itasca State Park, famous for the headwaters of the Mississippi River. Unfortunately, there was a huge stalled storm in that direction that thundered for a solid hour. We waited and wondered how our friends riding north of us were doing with heavy clouds and thunder also in that direction.With some trepidation from both the lateness and the weather, we headed towards Itasca asking each other "Is this is a good idea?" Areas of wet road and construction added to that feeling. Again, we pulled it off and were rewarded with a fantastic red sunset. Not all the plans for the day worked out though. Because of the rain delay, we were too late to ride the park's Wilderness Loop and also too late to have dinner at the Park's Douglas Lodge. We crossed the Mississippi river for the first time just north of Itasca, and the river was all of about 10 feet across.

The year-round Hosteling International Youth Hostel at Itasca is a beautifully restored log building which used to serve as park headquarters. Tom Cooper, the manager, knows me from my many rides that way including annual rides to Winnipeg and didn't seem too impressed by what we were doing.

"Does this bike trail really go 50 miles?" We had just left quiet County Road 6 and started down the new Paul Bunyan paved bike trail in Hackensack, Minnesota. Mile markers on the trail were counting down from 50. Areas south of Itasca are somewhat of a bicyclist's dream. Highway 71 towards Park Rapids has signs warning turning motorists to yield to bikes. From Park Rapids to Walker is Minnesota's first paved bike trail, the Heartland Trail, which recently got a new and wider surface. Nice and relatively quiet paved county roads wind around rolling hills and tree-lined lakes all over this region. Like the Heartland, the Paul Bunyan trail has a superb surface which may stay that way if the State sticks to its restriction against metal stud-using snowmobiles on paved trails.

Leaving the bike trail at Jenkins, we started through a maze of roads and lakes to find a campground where I've traditionally stopped for lunch on past north-bound Winnipeg trips. Trouble is we were going south. I was 95 percent sure we were going right but kept turning around to get a look at the road "from the other direction." I was hoping Tom would just assume I was doing my usual checking up on how he was doing and searching for vistas which would make good photos of the "biker in his surroundings." He started to worry when we turned off a minor two lane county road to take a more minor unmarked hill bypass. But we soon saw the parked RV's at Highview Campground, the lake, and home for the night. We had another beautiful sunset.

The next day was all quiet county roads through Crow Wing State Forest, past many lakes (Tom finally stopped counting them), and another crossing of the Mississippi, now about 25 feet across. In Deerwood, we ate in a "diner" resembling a trolley car. Our waitress was a pretty young woman with a name tag: Michelle, who we bantered with a bit. I think we were getting starved for human contact besides each other. More nice roads to Mille Lacs Lake, an inland sea about 60 miles around. Here, Tom started a new act which would stay with us the rest of the trip. After I got my carefully selected treat at the bakery, he started to grouse about how I always got the bigger one and made the clerk search for a bigger version of the one I got. Of course, I reciprocated whenever possible and thus was born the "Two Grumpy Old Bikers" act.

I wanted to make this day an epic one so the next into Minneapolis would be easy, and Tom agreed. We would surely then make it to Minneapolis the next day and then have two clear ones in the city to clean up, service the bikes, etc. So, Mora at 100 miles became the destination. Checking in the Chamber of Commerce/Tourist Info office about local campgrounds, we met Jerry Nelson. Jerry invited us to camp in his back yard and then decided that in the house was better. Jerry and Ronette were gracious hosts, and we felt like family with them. It also provided Tom with another audience, as he never seemed to tire of telling people about our travels. That night we went to a Chinese restaurant, and our waitress was another "Michelle." Feeling happy and silly, I told her about the Deerwood "Michelle" earlier in the day and asked if they were related.

Mora to Minneapolis is a straight shot down a main road with a good shoulder (Highway 65). To make it more interesting, we detoured through Bunker Hill Park and took a bike path and route which follows the Mississippi River from the Coon Rapids Dam County Park to downtown Minneapolis. When I turned into Hennepin Avenue and rode down what looked like the middle of the street, Tom wasn't sure what I was doing or that he wanted to follow. Even when he saw the painted bike lane lines, he wasn't too sure.

Through downtown safely, we took the chain of lakes bike paths and arrived at my home in southwest Minneapolis. I was elated, Seattle to Minneapolis sounded and felt pretty epic-like.

While waiting for my wife Dana to come home from work, we took everything off the bikes and started to clean them. "Dave, look at this." Tom is meticulous about his stuff and his new Cannondale had a problem. Cracks were developing in his rear wheel rim. Between every other spoke, the freewheel side ones of course, the Sun CR17A rims were starting to split. We would have to do more than just clean, oil, and change rear tires.

Spent two days in Minneapolis, squeezing in a big family dinner, two short rides with friends, and a party with the "Arrowheads". The big event, however, was the rebuilding of Tom's wheels for which we imposed ourselves on a friend and local Cannondale Dealer, Terry Osell. On a summer Saturday, the busiest of bike shop days, a pair of matching wheels were rebuilt with Mavic MA2 rims. Tom *had to* have a new rear one and was afraid to try to do the rest of our tour without also redoing the front.

Chapter 7

Heading to RAGBRAI and Points East

"You can't have a BLT as it isn't 11 and lunch is not yet being served." You would think a restaurant named Emma Crumbies would see that BLT ingredients are pretty close to "breakfast." Did get the BLT's and then proceeded into the too-hot day to continue our ride south. Bicycle routes directly south from the Twin Cities are at best fair, with too much development and too many paved roads which turn to dirt. Heading southwest from Minneapolis along the Minnesota River, we had our BLT's in Belle Plaine and then turned south towards Iowa.

It was hot and headwindy, and the two-day "rest" hadn't been good for us. We were weak, sluggish, and without any desire to push very hard. A pick-up approached and seemed to shadow us. I expected trouble until the driver leaned out to warn us about the weather. We had been watching the growing clouds and thunder to our southwest (the direction the weather comes from in Minnesota) and knew that we might soon be needing shelter. We soon did, and found it in the tiny town of St. Thomas, a park shelter being our port in the storm. Thought about the name and joked with Tom. Earlier we had come across "Tom's Royal Pizza" (I called it Tom's Tiny Pizza) and also O'Brien's Cafe (crabby and boffo waitress). Now we sheltered in "St. Thomas."

It cleared, considerably cooler, and we continued, feeling considerably stronger. In Le Center, we saw that the storm had been serious with tree limbs down all over town. I told Tom about wind storms in the spring which had knocked down hundreds and possibly thousands of large trees in Minneapolis and St. Paul. The weather this year had been crazy. Pulled into Lake Sakatah State Park, on another of Minnesota's bike trails. Vicious mosquitos drove us to our respective tents at dusk where I fell asleep listening to Minnesota Public Radio on my Walkman.

The next day's weather was a repeat. Rode, waited out a rainstorm, and then continued on. Entered Iowa, taking the obligatory Stateline photo and rode through Fertile to Clear Lake State Park. At the campground check in, another camper heard Tom complaining about being a tired old biker and "can't go any farther." He later saw us coming back (on bikes of course) from dinner in town and yelled something about it. Tom replied something about a "fast recovery."

The next day we would seek and find RAGBRAI, the 26th edition of the Register's Annual Great Bicycle Ride Across Iowa. We started out with breakfast in a "7-calendar" restaurant. According to "Blue Highways" by W. L. H. Moon, this should rate as a top-of-the-line gourmet experience. This one was only adequate. Then we rode what seemed all of Iowa looking for the 15,000 or so bikers. Problem was, I knew the previous day's and that night's overnight towns but not the route between them. As we headed south, I was *sure* we would have to intercept their route. While searching and riding through towns, people waved, yelled encouragement, or asked if we were lost. They thought we were lost RAGBRAIers. We finally saw the flow of bikes and plunged in. After only a few hundred yards, we came to a food stop and stopped.

Not five minutes later, the Arrowhead Team stopped there. With them were some new "Arrows" or at least new to me, Betty and her daughter Cheryl. Betty was 75. I told her about my friends Ralph and Laverne from Los Angeles who at 71 and 68, respectively, are still doing double centuries. Talking about riding styles, I gave Betty my "low gear and spin" speech which had had no positive impact on teenagers Sarah and Lisa. She said she would have to try it. Yes!!!

"Dave, your bike fell down," said one of our Arrowheads. This was to be a tiny understatement. Our first overnight with friends doing RAGBRAI and I was given this message upon returning from some local on-foot errand. Trying to ride back to town, I found my rear gear bent in at a funny angle, broken. Hung the bike from a swing set to look it over and I also found my rear wheel was seriously out of true. Had ridden 3,100 miles from Seattle to Eldora, Iowa, with no mechanical problems, and my bike is damaged while parked! Apparently, one of our Arrows (who shall be unnamed) was climbing on the trailer looking for something deep in its bowels. The trailer's cover slipped and then so did he (or vice versa), he knocked over the line of bikes leaning against the trailer, and then fell or stomped on them, specifically mine. I was a tiny bit upset but kept my cool. That is, I didn't physically attack him.

So what is the big deal? Bikes can be fixed, even in the middle of a cross-country tour. I was upset because almost nothing on my bike is standard or easily replaced. (Non-technos can skip the rest of this paragraph and the next one too.) The bike has 120 mm dropout spacing for a five speed freewheel, a custom-sized five-speed freewheel, an indexing SunTour long cage derailleur, and 27-inch wheels. I had just built that rear wheel 100 miles before the start of the cross-country tour, and I am used to my wheels lasting 20,000 miles and more. I trued the wheel up as best I could and rode carefully and slowly to the main campground to consult with the shop mechanics presiding there. Tom went with me as a calming influence. It was already dark, and the mechanics looked like they could drop from exhaustion at any minute. Got a commitment from the folks at Bike World of Des Moines to work on it the following day and they advised me to get there early. Not wanting a break in the cross-country tour, I rode carefully to the next overnight town. Had to avoid the largest freewheel cog as the cage was hanging at an angle and could have been caught by the spokes.

Repair prognosis: $185 worth! They replaced the derailleur with a Shimano LX. Amazingly, it still index shifted using the SunTour down tube shift levers, a kind of miracle! The old rim had a permanent kink. They had no 27-inch rims (no big surprise) but found a 700C with 36 spoke holes. This was a Mavic MA2 rim, the same kind Tom now had on his bike. Was a little nervous about this rim as it is narrower and possibly less stiff than the ones I was used to using for loaded touring, Super Champion Model 58's. They carefully rebuilt and trued that wheel under a hot sun and I was apparently ready to continue. Being very busy, they did not offer and I did not ask them to rebuild the front wheel. So I finished the 5,500 mile cross-country tour with one 700C and one 27-inch wheel. To their credit, that wheel stayed perfectly true for the remaining 2,400 miles and did not even need the usual 100-mile "adjustment."

RAGBRAI has been written up in many articles and is known as a fun event where many riders are in thematic teams and don't take themselves too seriously. However, it's a *crowded* fun event which I wasn't sure Tom would like. We had a lot invested in our half-done cross-country tour and wanted no disaster to prematurely end it. At our ages, it is not certain that we would get another try.

Rode, camped, partied, ate, explained the "arrows," met old friends, and did the last three days of the week-long event with about 20,000 other bicyclists. One of those was an old friend, Eileen McDeid from Clinton, Iowa. I had met Eileen and her kids Rowan and Bryce in 1977 on my first-time RAGBRAI ride with the Lake Country Cyclists. This year, she and a friend Ron were riding on their new Easy Tour recumbents. After RAGBRAI, Tom and I were going to swing south and east to rejoin the Adventure Cycling Northern Tier route. Clinton was a convenient overnight in this direction and Eileen was gracious enough to let us invite ourselves to stop there.

Clinton

Odell

Bradford

Rensselaer

Salamonie River

ILLINOIS

INDIANA

100 miles

Chapter 8

Across the Heartland

Saturday, the last day of RAGBRAI, was about 75 miles. Up and down the scenic Mississippi bluffs, the last day is always a bit sad as everyone contemplates returning to the "real world" outside of RAGBRAI. Said our goodbyes to our Arrowhead friends packing for their drive back to the Twin Cities. Tom and I then rode south on the Illinois side of the Mississippi River to a bridge where we could cross into Clinton, Iowa. We had only asked to camp in Elieen's yard but were not too surprised to be invited in the house. The next day, Eileen and Ron rode with us via river bike paths to Albany, Ilinois, for breakfast, after which we then said more goodbyes. Finally, Tom and I were again heading east and alone.

Near Kewanee, Illinois, we again picked up the Adventure Cycling's Northern Tier route which we had left so long ago, it seemed, in Devils Lake, North Dakota. Somehow, we expected to see other coast-to-coast bikers around every bend and rise and indeed did meet one within a few miles. He was an anomaly, however, bike touring but not coast-to-coast, nor did he even know about the Adventure Cycling route and maps. Unlike in the West, we were pretty much the lone cyclists and decided it was because bikers had many choices in the East: our route, Upper Michigan, or by ferry across Lake Michigan.

Illinois, Indiana, and western Ohio surprised us. We had been hearing about how hot it had been there earlier in the summer and I expected the area to be miles of sweat and either scary or boring roads. Instead, the Adventure Cycling maps directed us through a maze of nice back roads through flat to gently rolling and attractive countryside which reflected the pride of the farmers. Some areas were still flooded from recent monster storms but most were planted and well advanced for the season. Corn was eight and more feet high and some borders between the road and crops were beautifully mowed grass. We could ride along easy in the warm tail winds and talk about our previous lives and the philosophy of it all.

The towns were also surprises but a mixed bag. Our first overnight in Illinois was Bradford. It was about the right distance of 83 miles and a larger town. But, the Adventure Cycling map said nothing about camping there. We searched for and finally contacted local authority who said the town park was not appropriate but we could camp out of sight behind the school. The only place to eat on a Sunday was a Casey's convenience store which had a pizza take-out service. We ordered one and took it down the main street to the corner park to sit and eat on this nice warm summer evening. It was one of those memorable meals. While we were eating, one boy and one girl of about 14 came over and sat next to us to ask about our travels. They were mildly interested in us. We lost our interest in them very quickly as the boy periodically spit out a juicy wad on the ground between him and us and the girl described her narrow view of life and how it should be led. They were not an attractive pair. Well, it was *their* town and *their* park, but it did take the edge off our appetite.

Those two told us about the "bad" kids, known to egg and spray-paint tents of bikers staying in the town. Some slightly older youths came past to shoot some hoops. The spitter said these weren't the "bad kids" and then yelled to one, "These guys biked all the way from Seattle." The immediate response was "That's dumb." The vehemence and conviction behind that response left us a little speechless. We had no interest in lecturing any of those kids but it got us talking later about the narrow and sad lives these kids live. Their ambitions are to get out of that town and to get a car (or better yet, a truck). Bike riding of any kind is "dumb," and riding across the country must be the greatest "dumb" possible. They act macho and all-knowing.

After eating as much of that pizza as we could stomach, we gave the rest away and biked over to the school behind which we had earlier pitched our two tents. We didn't get there right away, however. In the small lot in front were about a dozen kids, talking, milling around, smoking, getting in and out of cars and racing around the town and returning. Were these the "bad" kids? Rather than going to our tents behind the school and revealing their location, we pulled up to the throng and engaged them in conversation. They spoke about their dislike of the town and specifically the local authority. We thought: "the bad kids." In any event, we did not ask them about their throwing or painting skills, but just hung around and vaguely and untruthfully answered questions about where we were staying. I did not sleep well that night.

Donuts from Casey's provided our pre-breakfast. They were better than last night's pizza. Rolled into Henry, Illinois, an attractive riverside town. Found real breakfasts and postcards that featured the Henry school, swimming pool, church, a local factory, etc. They were black and white and cheap and we bought lots of them. I was still sending "Henry" postcards in Indiana. It was a nice day as we rode and talked about Bradford, its kids, and what that says about rural America, our country and its youth. We also bantered about the idea that this trip was "dumb." In some ways it was. However, how will that ball hooper describe his "adventure-filled" summer? No doubt he'll write a book about it.

That night we were in Odell, Ilinois, a town much different than Bradford. The downtown looked more vibrant, and there was none of the menacing feeling we had in Bradford. People we spoke to seemed friendly. We showered in the city pool (free) and camped in the park next to it (also free). Riding around later, I discovered that Odell was on old Route 66 and there were old signs and buildings from that era. One of Tom's dreams is to follow that road from Chicago to the Santa Monica Pier. Parts of old 66 that I had biked on near Rolla, Missouri, weren't in very good shape where they were there at all. The Wishing Well cafe was a real treat and was run by people from Macedonia, once part of Yugoslavia. They seemed more like Greeks to me aside from fitting the stereotype that restaurants are run by Greeks and that Macedonia is an ancient name for Greece.

Continued on across the narrow part of Illinois toward Indiana. Enjoyed the light work load the tail winds made but not their contribution to the considerable heat. Traffic was both light and courteous on the mostly back roads across the border and on to Rensselaer, Indiana. This bigger town has a college and a large downtown. Finding the park and swimming took us awhile. Here, the pool personnel were again very nice. We put away the "grumpy" act for awhile. Later while doing laundry, Tom and I tied in a Ben & Jerry's ice cream eating contest. I choose "Dilbert" flavor which was nutty and seemed to have chunky pieces of cubicle in it.

Our first full day in Indiana did not live up to our expectations. Head winds and road detours slowed us a bit, and the closest town to our destination, Lagro, was worse than Bradford, Illinois. Most of the downtown was boarded up, and young males yelled at us from both street corners and cars. The overnight camp site had seemed better than reality too. We rode to the Salamonie River State Forest Campgrounds which was pretty enough. However, we craved showers and there were none there or nearby, nor anything to eat. We ended up riding back to Lagro, eating there, washing ourselves in a gas station, and then riding back once again to the campground. If we had known or planned better, we could have eaten in Lagro the first time through and done one ride to the far eastern reaches of the Salamonie Forest where there was supposed to be a better equipped campground. With all the back and forth, we had gone 110 miles that day. High Five, for the distance at least.

Felt dirty and sticky the next morning as we portaged a road washout in the park and detoured to the relatively large city of Huntington, Indiana. Apparently, that portaging had broken off a tab on Tom's pedal cleat, which was then imperfectly attached to his clipless pedal. We hoped to get a replacement in Huntington. After a great breakfast served at a corner cafe, we found the only bike shop in town which didn't look likely to have the clete Tom needed. But we had detoured there and it would only be an hour till it opened, or so the sign said. It was 1-1/2 hours (11 a.m.) when the owner pulled in. As we feared, no shoe cleat. Tom then phoned his shop in Portland to send a pair to my cousin Marty whom we would see in a few days in Cleveland, Ohio.

Our long wait in Huntington and head winds made it late when we pulled into Paulding, Ohio, via Zanesville, Indiana (and friendly college student Holly in the general store). The Paulding policeman was nice but adamant that there was nowhere to camp in or close to town. He suggested a bargain motel, and we decided to "treat" ourselves at $30 for two persons. Also treated ourselves to McDonald's sundaes. A poor second to Ben & Jerry's but tasty enough and lots cheaper.

Western Ohio was more easy terrain. We passed homes on large grassy tracts, many of which had their own ponds in front and looked like miniature golf courses. The route followed the Auglaize River to Defiance. We took a quick look around this historic town where the Auglaize joins the Maumee. We then continued along the Maumee to Napoleon, which, like many Midwest county seats, has a spectacular old courthouse. Across from the square, we found a nice old restaurant, Spenglers with one wall painted "Established 1879." Our server said the town had recently hosted a giant horde of bicyclists. We assumed it was the GTE Big Tour. After lunch, we rode through heavy traffic around Bowling Green and on to Pemberville. We later heard people affectionately refer to Bowling Green as "BG." From our memory of passing through on bikes, BG meant more like "Big Golldarn Traffic."

Pemberville had to be our dinner stop, as our planned overnight was an isolated rural campground 10 miles farther on. We also visited the local bike shop and met an interesting guy with a hobby of designing specialized bike tools. I tried to buy some bicycling gloves but he insisted on giving them away to both of us. Said he doesn't have any customers for them. Tom and I couldn't believe he would have enough customers to support a bike shop in such a small town. The Cactus Flat campground was an amiable place but was all RV's and had no showers. Cleaned up the best we could but were grateful the day hadn't been too hot.

The next day was the first of August and we were starting to be aware of the coming end-of-trip. We had been on the road since June 12 (50 days) and only had about 18 more. In talking with people at about this stage of the trip, we described out goal as "Coast of Maine" and said "we were almost there." That invariably drew smiles and sometimes shaking heads. I am sure people in Ohio, Pennsylvania, etc. do not consider themselves as living in "almost Maine." But for us, this was the case. We had gone about 4,000 miles by July 31 and had only about a thousand left. With all our memories of all the places we had been, we felt like we were truly "almost there."

We detoured to Fremont, Ohio, for breakfast and then got back on the route. Had a repeat of the day before with similar nice back roads, another college town (Oberlin), an afternoon ice cream break, and a dinner stop before the end-of-the-day ride to camp. We had mild head winds on this 101-mile day and Tom was going slow, nursing a knee which was swelling again as it had a few days earlier. Dinner was in Grafton, and thankfully, the Maples Campground a few miles farther on had showers! Like Cactus Flats the day before, the Maples was in an isolated rural setting and we had to ride nearly 20 hungry miles for breakfast. In Brunswick, a western suburb of Cleveland and right on our route, we found an unlikely looking place, a bar called the Red Onion. I had to push on the door to tell if it was open. The place was a hit.

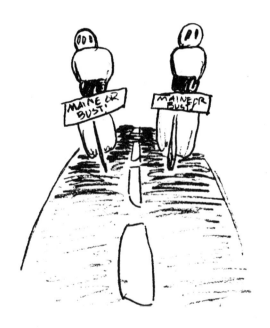

LEFT
Tom O'Brien, fully loaded at trip's start.
BOTTOM
Tom Smith, Tom O'Brien and the author,
in Anacortes, Washington,
the official beginning of the
cross-country trip

ABOVE
Tom Smith and the tame rabbits at
Marblemount camp ground.
LEFT
Tom O'Brien approaching
Washington Pass in the
Northern Cascades

ABOVE
Breakfast at Sam's Place in
wild-west town of Winthrop, WA.
LEFT
Downside of Washington Pass,
North Cascades of Washington State.
BELOW
Author reviewing indispensable
Adventure Cycling map.

ABOVE
Dry hills of eastern Washington State.
BELOW LEFT
Pig in western Montana bar/restaurant near turnoff to Bull River valley.
BELOW RIGHT
Bridge over Pend Oreille River to Usk, WA

ABOVE
Sarah, Scott, Lisa and Ann Weigle from
Bainbridge Island, WA.
LEFT
Tom approaching storm in Bull River
valley in western Montana.
BELOW
"Two guys and a girl." Ken, Ron and
Karen from Michigan.

ABOVE
Tom O'Brien consulting his watch at the start of the climb to Logan Pass, the
"Going-to-the-Sun Highway" in Glacier National Park.
BELOW
Going-to-the-Sun-Highway, just reopened after heavy snow.

ABOVE
Glacier Park mountains receding in the distance behind Tom.
BELOW
Approaching the prairie and railroad city of Havre, Montana.

ABOVE
Cenex station somewhere in North Dakota.
Nine bicyclists from five different "teams"
who have converged as part of the
fellowship of the road.
L to R: Scott, Tom, Dave, Sarah,
Lisa, Mike, the Author, Jason, and Julia.
LEFT
Jason Snell from Michigan and
his "home" on the road.

TOP LEFT
Headwaters of the Mississippi River is Itasca Lake in northern Minnesota.
TOP RIGHT
"Paul Bunyan" in Akeley, Minnesota. Guardian of bicyclists.
BOTTOM
Downtown Minneapolis Sculpture Garden. We're halfway there.

ABOVE
RAGBRAI, ride across Iowa is neither boring nor is it "flat".
For one week, bikers rule the road.
BELOW
Midwest cornfield and manicured grass shoulder in Illinois.

ABOVE LEFT
Vermont covered bridge.
ABOVE RIGHT
Only in Maine can a sign such as this be found.
BELOW
One of nearly 60 campsites on the nine-week ride.

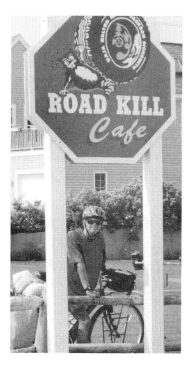

ABOVE
The gear is back in the campground and the bikers
are at Ocean point near Boothbay Harbor, Maine.
RIGHT
We could not try every restaurant en route.
BELOW
The Youth Hostel in Boston on the
day of departure for home at trip's end.

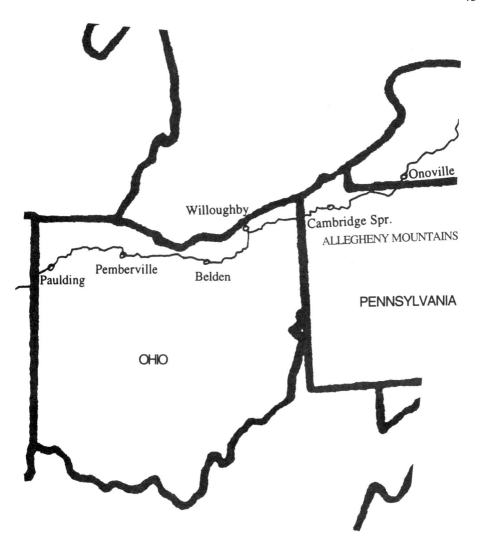

Onoville

Willoughby

Cambridge Spr.

ALLEGHENY MOUNTAINS

Pemberville

Belden

Paulding

PENNSYLVANIA

OHIO

100 miles

Chapter 9

The Alleghenys, Adirondacks, and the End of "Bicycling Light"

Upon entering the Cleveland area, we started to encounter heavy and hectic eastern traffic, which would pretty much characterize the rest of the trip. That is when we also realized how enjoyable the roads had been between southern Minnesota and central Ohio. We also started encountering constant hills, another companion for the remainder. There was great beauty but there was also much work to travel it.

To most people, Cleveland does not conjure up thoughts of woods and hills. However, Adventure Cycling's route travels Cleveland's "Emerald Necklace" park system which has plenty of both. (Note: The route in this area was redesigned in 1999 to follow the shore of Lake Erie.) Approaching the parkway, we turned a corner onto Cato Street and faced a short but very steep climb with both busy traffic and a rough surface. I'm not sure what happened, but, I expect that Tom waited too long to shift into his granny gear. He had to dismount and walk. This really bummed him out after negotiating the Cascades, Glacier Park's Going-To-The-Sun Highway, etc. He said he hasn't had to walk a hill in many years.

We traveled the park's bike path system on this hot and humid day. I am on the Board of a professional society (ISEE), which has its home office only one mile from the Parkway. We stopped there but no one was around on a Sunday. Tom took my picture sitting on their address sign. The road along the Chagrin River was especially nice, but we could not enjoy it much with the heavy Sunday traffic on the narrow pavement and spots of new sticky tar repairs.

Our destination was my cousin Marty Siskind's house in Willoughby, only a few miles off the AC route. When I told Marty we would be passing nearby and invited ourselves to stop there, he asked if we needed to be *picked up*. We laughed at the thought that we couldn't do a detour of three or four miles on a trip of over

5,000. We were a day up on schedule at this point, which was lucky as Sunday was family get-together night for the Ohio Siskinds. Tom and I went with Marty. I met cousins never met before and we both enjoyed the evening, although somewhat tired from the hilly, hot, and humid day. Tom had lots of new people to tell our trip stories to.

Monday: Marty had to go to work and Tom and I had to go to Pennsylvania. We had breakfast with Marty in a local Bob Evans, took pictures, and then headed east with some creekside and shaded roads and lots more hills. I saw a sign at the Ohio/Pennsylvania border that I misread at first glance. I thought it said "Keep Pennsylvania Beautiful, Do Not Enter." Actually, it said "Do Not Litter." We were on the Allegheny Plateau, a feeling I knew well from my six years at Penn State in State College. Every town was in a valley and every road between them via a big climb. It was beautiful country but too hazy for spectacular photography.The Adventure Cycling route across Pennsylvania cuts the northwest corner south of Erie, and we would only have one overnight in that State. Our goal of 100 miles made that Cambridge Springs, Pennsylvania.

This attractive town had lots of old bar-restaurants, but we had dinner in a new place, the Cross Bow. During dinner, we were asked about our travels (the bikes were parked outside the window), and Tom told his usual stories. When it came time to pay, it was "on the house." Thank you, Carla. Later, Tom walked over to the campground office at Mitchell Lake to pay for our site and came back with "Guess how much?" It was also "on the house." There sure is good karma for bikers in Cambridge Springs. That goes double as we had also done laundry there and both of us had panniers full of clean clothes, "happy panniers."

We would make it to New York State the next day. Before then, we traveled more Pennsylvania hills and had lunch in Corry. There, I was ogled. Now, at 56, I don't expect this even though I am reasonably trim and fit. Walking into the restaurant, which will not be identified, I got the two full looks up and down. Admittedly, I had on my tight bright-red Descent bike jersey, zipper down, and tight bike shorts. The attractive waitress also asked if we were staying in town (unfortunately or perhaps fortunately, "no.") Why didn't such things happen when I lived in Pennsylvania and was

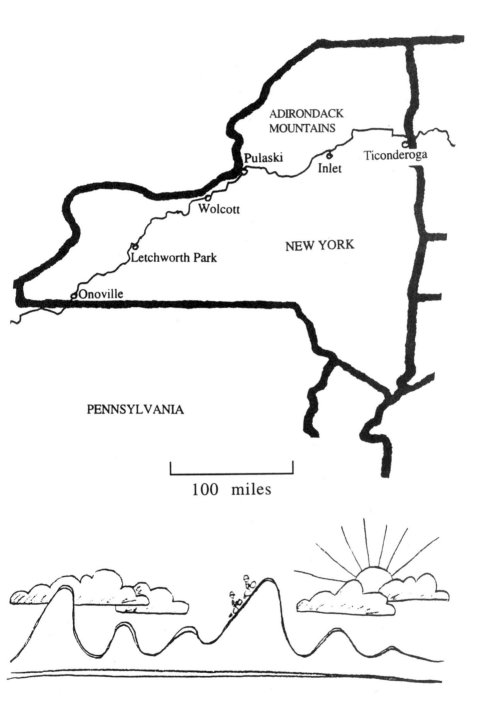

100 miles

single for 25 years? This was all wrong anyway; after all, I was still hoping to find Karen. Besides, all this, including Karen, was a lot of fantasy. I probably should have been abashed, but I did get a thrill out of the "look." Apparently, women don't these days, considering it threatening or demeaning. Perhaps my age had something to do with it.

We continued on, reluctantly, after I bought another new water bottle at a local bike shop. The old one, from Minot, North Dakota, was growing algae. Our destination was Onoville, New York, on the Allegheny Reservoir. We celebrated our recent State-a-day progress with a nice dinner in the Red Wing restaurant served by beautiful Amy. At this point, all the women we were seeing were beautiful, but Amy *really* was.

By then we were getting a little tired of hills and wondering if Adventure Cycling could have found slightly easier back roads. Our State map showed old Highway 17 along the river and through the Indian reservation. This would have gotten us from Steamburg to Salamanca from which we could turn north and pick up the Adventure Cycling route again in Ellicottville, all valley riding. We asked in the restaurant and were told the old road was still there. It was, but, the top two-inch layer was irregularly broken and/or missing, slowing us to an effective safe speed of five mph. We tried it and then turned back and bit the bullet (rode the hills).

Our second strategy was more radical and more successful. I knew from a trip in this area the previous year (going Philadelphia to Minneapolis) that the hills decreased in upstate New York. The Adventure Cycling route stays south until Watkins Glen and then turns north between two of the Finger Lakes. It is undoubtedly scenic, but we were ready for a sacrifice. We turned north sooner, leaving the Adventure Cycling route at Portageville and camping at beautiful Letchworth State Park. It was too late to see the park's natural beauty, but the store did have ice cream.

We continued north the next day through Geneseo and to the vicinity of Rochester, where we picked up Highway 31 along the Erie Canal. Northward riding was easier as it followed the "lay of the land." Seeing the historic canal was interesting, but traffic in the Rochester area resembled a disturbed hornets nest. Being off the Adventure Cycling map, we had a harder time finding campgrounds but found one near Wolcott, just south of, but not within sight of, Lake Ontario.

Somewhere around here we had a couple of funny dog experiences. Our usual reactions are that I yell at them and Tom just yells. Apparently, there are fewer bike-chasing dogs in Portland than where I usually ride in Minnesota and Wisconsin. One day we were cruising in our usual formation, Tom a few bike-lengths behind me, when a tiny dog ran across his yard and launched himself off the four- or five-foot-high embankment. He landed on his feet and on the run and continued the chase. I caught this out of the corner of my eye, was kind of astounded, but just continued at my same sedate 15 mph. Tom almost died laughing. It was a circus-type performance.

The second incident followed this by a few days. Same riding formation but different lawn. Again I saw this in my peripheral vision: a big shaggy dog running across the yard, tripping and tumbling in a roadside ditch. He somehow didn't break his neck, got up, and resumed chasing me. I continued to cruise but soon noticed an inordinate amount of commotion behind me. A fully grown woman was chasing the dog who was chasing me. She was yelling as the three of us paraded on. I felt sorry for her while also being amazed she could sustain 15 mph for so long. I finally stopped dead and watched her catch and throttle the poor mutt. Tom again laughed.

We were ready for an easy day after a string of four hard centuries. So, we set a goal for Pulaski, New York, at the southeast corner of Lake Ontario. This was less than 60 miles, back on the Adventure Cycling route, and at the threshold of the Adirondacks. Selkirk Shores State park was full but the Bears Sleepy Hollow RV park next door was nice and accommodated us. We had ignored a few rain drops this day as they just didn't seem sufficiently threatening. Traffic was threatening, however, as it was a Friday and there was a heavy stream of cars from the south (presumably the New York City area). Another negative was that none of the pay phones in this area seemed to work although they accepted money without problem. It was also hot and humid. Okay, this is the East and crankiness is pervasive.

Our two days in the Adirondacks were characterized as scenic, not too busy, and with more pleasant weather. The coolness and lower humidity made both of us feel less lethargic. We were now out of the Alleghenys and in "real" mountains. However, they seemed far more benign. They went up for a long time and then they went down for a long time. Not the hard trudge followed by the crazy rush, repeated frequently and ad infinitum. We talked about those northwest Pennsylvania and southwest New York hills. It takes 1/2 hour to 45 minutes to climb one of them and 5 minutes to descend. Allowing a few minutes of level ground at the crest and in the hollow means that 75 to 90 pct of the day's time is spent climbing. No wonder we were getting fatigued.

Approaching our planned lunch stop in West Leyden, New York, we caught up with two on single bikes, Bob and Marge Thomas from Boise, Idaho. We had heard that there were bikers ahead of us, including a tandeming couple, and thought the tandem might be Dick and Marilyn from Sacramento with their Bob Trailer. The first thing we found out is that the Thomases had met and ridden with Scott and the girls near Rochester, New York. The small world of the long-distance bike tourist. They were also going coast to coast but planning to continue on to Nova Scotia, Canada. We four had lunch together and then separated as Tom and I had a more ambitious schedule.

We stayed that night in Limekiln Lake State Park, a few hilly miles off the route. The park was crowded, but the officials were nice and found space for us. We also noticed that the park seemed to be beat from overuse. We completed our crossing of the Adirondacks the next day with better scenic views of hills and lakes, and a fast descent into Ticonderoga near Lake Champlain. The humidity had returned, and we were tired with 105 miles on the clock. We were also energized as tomorrow was not only another State but another "world," New England.

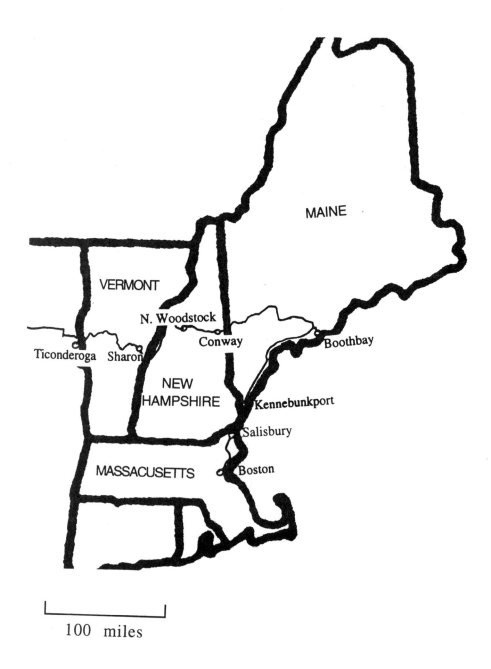

MAINE

VERMONT

N. Woodstock

Conway

Boothbay

Ticonderoga   Sharon

NEW
HAMPSHIRE

Kennebunkport

Salisbury

MASSACUSETTS

Boston

100 miles

Chapter 10

The Land of Small States

The ferry took us across to Vermont, a beautiful and civilized State: the road sign greeting us said "Speed Limit is 50 mph Unless Posted Otherwise." Unfortunately, the high humidity had returned and I was completely lacking in pep. Tom seemed less affected. Almost immediately, Adventure Cycling gave us a route decision: a short ride on a gravel road leading to a covered bridge or longer ride on all pavement through a fair sized town. We choose the gravel. It and the bridge were quite acceptable. The Adventure Cycling route took us to East Middlebury and over the Green Mountains to Hancock where we lunched. The climb was long and steep, and we were totally covered with sweat.

I temporarily lost Tom after a bank stop and we had some separate but equal adventures ducking rain showers. We found each other at an ice cream stop and then continued on, dodging puddles to Sharon, Vermont. This was short of Thetford, our goal. Between our tiredness, the rain, and searching for each other, we were ready to call it a day and crash in the local hotel. Unbelievably, I became more energized after dinner and cooling off and I rode another 22 mostly riverside miles to clock up a day total of 103.

It was raining at dawn but stopped by 10 a.m. We were "psyched out" about the climb to Thetford, the stretch we had declined to do the day before. Instead, we went down the White River to West Lebanon, New Hampshire, where we turned north to arrive at Thetford by following the Connecticut River. On "paper" it looked like a better choice, but wasn't. It was certainly a longer way to get there. Also, New Hampshire Highway 10 was inland instead of hugging the river shoreline and quite rolling. One plan was that, if the rain resumed, we could have stopped at the Youth Hostel in White River Junction. After lunch in Thetford, we continued on the Adventure Cycling route, dodged a short rain shower at, of all places, an ice cream stand, and pulled in to North Haverhill. There, we discussed strategy and decided that North Woodstock over a "small mountain" was within reach. Interpreting the map, I figured that we would climb a shoulder of Black Mountain and then cruise downhill along the Wild Ammonoosue River to North Woodstock.

Well, we climbed the shoulder as expected and descended to the Wild Ammonoosue. Problem: the Wild Amm was flowing in the wrong direction! We weren't going to cruise anywhere without first going up a long climb, the top of which was way out of sight. I was kind of meek over this map misreading. Fortunately, it wasn't steep, the road was quiet, wide, and very smooth (newly paved), and we climbed easily. On the climb, we crossed the Appalachian Trail, and Tom took a few steps on it for the camera. At Kinsman Notch were surprises of both sight and sound. The sight was the road plunging into the abyss between the mountain we were on and the series of White Mountain ranges facing us. The sound was one short grunt from Tom: "Wow," as he disappeared down that abyss. I stopped a second to take a photo of his rapidly disappearing back and then started down myself. The road was so smooth and the air so quiet that I was amazed at my first glance at my computer: 48 mph. In a tight tuck, I passed Tom at 51 mph, a personal record by one mph. North Woodstock is totally touristville but we were very happy with our day considering the weather and our late start.

Morning and threatening skies. We did not know what our next day's destination was but we knew we faced Kancamagus Pass through the White Mountains. A trip to this area of New Hampshire (Pinkham Notch) in 1984 resulted in the thought, "Dave, you're getting too old for this." Well, I am a lot older now and here again with a friend who is "really old" (just kidding, Tom). Fortunately, we were more experienced or just too determined, or perhaps, (and most likely) this pass is easier than Pinkham. It wasn't bad even with a rain storm chasing us down the eastern side to Conway, NH. There we resumed our usual strategy: ducking out of it in an ice cream shop.

The rain didn't stop so we decided to, at a fortunately-placed Youth Hostel in that very town. While waiting, I found a barber and got one wild trim. In retrospect, I should have waited for one more week and home. The Hostel was really nice, had laundry equipment, and a place to clean up and oil the bikes. Dinner was at a fish restaurant across the town's old covered bridge. Tomorrow was Maine, our "there" of "we are almost there."

After all the rain from mid-Vermont on, clear and cold was a nice change. This was one of our epic days, across the State of Maine in one day of 118 miles. We had decided to make Boothbay Harbor our Maine (and main) destination. We could have easily made Bar Harbor, the Adventure Cycling coastal end-point. But that could have complicated our getting to Boston where we were to rendezvous with our mass transportation, especially if the bad weather returned. Boothbay was far enough north that we would see the rocky coast of Maine and still make an easily manageable ride to Boston. We followed the Adventure Cycling route to Norway, Maine where we took an urban shortcut through Auburn and Lewiston. This saved us a half-dozen miles and some hills, and returned us to the Adventure Cycling route at Sabattus.

Maine is a nice State, and urban riding there seemed relatively safe. We had half expected another "Rochester, New York". At Dresden, we left the Adventure Cycling route for the last time as we turned southeast towards Boothbay. The little Ponderosa camp ground was our home in Boothbay, about five miles short of the harbor and the seashore. We saved that last bit for the next day.

Chapter 11

The Seashore and The End of The Road.

Our schedule allowed us a day off, which we used to explore every inlet and peninsula around Southport and Boothbay Harbor and photograph ourselves at every beach, pier, and overlook. We were at the same time elated and deflated. Even with three days of coastal riding remaining, we were "there." The "goal" had been reached, and we were faced with our personal "end of the road." We kept saying "We made it," and also thought privately "What's next?" The big ride was over but the "bigger" ride of life goes on. Before riding into town, we wrote "Tom and Dave" in soap on the road shoulder with an arrow pointing to the campground. We had known that Scott and the girls were somewhere on the Maine coast and thought they might pass by while we were there. (Found out later they were too far north at this time. See Postscript)

We returned in the dark to camp at the end of our 40-mile "day off" to the news that the owner had been waiting for us and had arranged for a Boothbay Register reporter to interview us. Of course, Tom had talked about our trip when we checked in. The campground owner thought it a big event for Boothbay, unlike Bar Harbor where lots of bikers must finish. It was too late by then for the reporter. Instead, the owner and his wife interviewed us and asked us to stop at the office for a photo in the morning before we left. (We were subjects of a nice and accurate article Sept. 3, 1998, along with a companion article about a local bicyclist, Roger Carlson from Southport. Carlson had ridden the 3,254-mile GTE Big Ride and said "he's glad he did it but wouldn't do it again". The article about Roger was one of challenge, adversity, drama, etc. Look for his book in your local bookstore.)

We left Boothbay to travel the Coast of Maine south towards Boston with an intermediate stop in New Hampshire. U.S. Highway 1 was very busy, and we were seeing loaded bikers heading north, none of whom stopped to visit and talk. With the heavy traffic, there was reluctance on anyone's part to dash across the road. The natural bicyclist's companionship we felt on the coast-to-coast trip just wasn't there. The police threw us off of U.S. 1 near Bath and we had to negotiate other streets until south of Brunswick. Tom had noticed the "no bikers" sign but I was heads-down rushing forward and was thereupon chased down and sirened off the road. It was all very confusing with I-95 in the area and U.S. 1 turning into bikeless expressways for short distances and then reverting back.

In Freeport, we encountered hordes of people and many large buildings. Being away from home so long, I had forgotten about all the catalogs that would be awaiting my return. Among them would be several from L. L. Bean, from Freeport, Maine. Realization dawned. We left town as fast as we could pedal, as the crowds made us uncomfortable. Went through Portland where I took Tom's picture feigning a confused state as he lives in another Portland. According to Tom, the Oregon one was settled by people from the Maine one. More relaxing was the beach road through Old Orchard.

We stayed in Salty Acres campground near Cape Porpoise, just short of Kennebunk, Maine. This was a busy tourist place, and the local mostly seafood restaurants did not appeal to us. So we found a pizza restaurant that was cheap and okay until it filled with some families with teams of young, restless, and noisy kids. To add to the din, they had a TV on and the kids took over the remote. We finally escaped, wondering if we had just surpassed the previous pizza trauma of note, Bradford, Illinois (Chapter 7). I needed a ride after that, plus 20 more miles. Down the road was Kennebunkport, bustling and interesting and, I later remembered, the summer home of past President George Bush. Took a photo of what I assumed was the Bush residence, a sprawling modern home on an isolated peninsula, and rode back to camp.

Heavy rain predicted for the night never came and the day dawned clear. Passed the Bush residence with Tom and found breakfast in Kennebunkport at a restaurant with the weirdest salt shakers. Every set on every table was different and very kitsch. After breakfast, we were able to get off of U.S. 1 and onto nice rolling roads through woods and along the shore. We saw other, presumably local, riders carrying no gear on their bikes.

We entered Portsmith, New Hampshire. It felt strange to be back in New Hampshire, which has only a few miles of Atlantic Ocean shoreline. We left U.S. 1 again for the shore and found that Rye

Beach was nice but Hampton Beach pandemonium. It was a summer Sunday, and everyone east of the Mississippi and not driving in the White Mountains was there. We viewed the spectacle awhile then departed for a quieter Salisbury Beach and its State Reservation. In contrast to Hampton, this looked like the aftermath of war with boarded up shops and closed amusement parks. We had to backtrack a few miles to find dinner. The campground lacked good grass and my attempt to find some put me too close to my neighbor's fire-ring, which he promised would be illuminating. Had to pull stakes and drag the tent to the far side of our site. Our other neighbor had trouble with her kid's plastic swimming pool and flooded the area. We were between fire and water.

We got out of there at first light for what was supposed to be an easy 40-mile ride into Boston. I had visited Boston before and seconded an old cyclist friend's suggestion that the State should be called "Nastychussetts." It wasn't bad at first even though we were on a beeline down U.S. 1. The sky was threatening, and we did not want to chance a circuitous route. We also noticed that I-95 paralleled U.S. 1 close by and should have most of the traffic. Left U.S. 1 for Beverly and Salem and, just beyond, the skies opened up. First we stopped at an animal shelter, but the barking was worse that a room full of pizza-eating kids. During a brief lull, we found an overhang at a supermarket in Lynn. This was our "home" for the next four hours or so as the rain turned into a gully washer and never quit. We should have stayed at the animal shelter. This supermarket had both the oddest customers and the oddest employees. A security man kept coming out and watching us with suspicious sideways glances. He somehow knew we planned to steal all the boxes of Hefty bags to make a tunnel from Lynn to Boston. We waited, trying to stay out of everyone's way. Every half-hour or so, we went in to buy something.

A local told us that there is a commuter train into Boston and that they take bikes in off hours. Rather than riding the mile or so in the pouring rain to the station, we tried to call them from the market to verify that we could get to Boston that way. Trouble is, neither we nor anyone else at the market's assistance desk could find the transit company in the phone book. After a half hour of looking, we suited up and rode the wet distance. Found the station easily and carried the bikes up two flights of steps. Soon a train came. A fellow on the platform said permits for bikes are usually required. He also said they will usually allow exceptions and it is up to the conductor. We were hoping for the exception but didn't get it. The doors opened and we barely said a word (nicely) when the conductor went ballistic, yelling about his job being on the line or something similar, and the nearly empty train pulled away without us. Ponder. Should we wait for the next one and try again or just give up and slosh into Boston? We decided to slosh and carried the loaded bikes down the steps and off the platform, thinking "Nastychussetts."

Automatic protection against suffering wiped away most of the memory of that ride. The roads got very busy as we approached Boston, and puddles were everywhere. Tom, in position behind me, thought the cars were swerving closer as they passed to effect a better splash. Nastychussetts. I couldn't keep the map out as it would have turned to wet matzo. So we got lost. First, biking in the Boston area and around its rivers and harbors requires creative navigation, as many main roads and bridges don't allow bikes. Second, the ones that do, do strange things like disappearing underground (Massachusetts Highway 99). There was a certain reluctance to follow them in the heavy traffic and rain as they plunged into dark tunnels. Crossing a bridge, we passed a walker and I got a "yes" to my question "Is this Boston?" Well, close but no prize. Nothing on the map matched the street signs and the sun was not visible. It was still raining. We wandered around about an hour before someone told us we were in *Cambridge*. Found another bridge, Boston, and the bike path along the correct side of the Charles River. It still took a few times around the block to find the Hostel in the confusing maze of wet, busy, and honking traffic streets. The Hostel was a pandemonium of people trying to check in, but it had a dry basement workshop where, upon cleaning ourselves and regaining some semblance of humanity, we cleaned our bikes.

The long day and my interaction with the Boston transit system weren't quite over. The same transit company that operates trains you can't take also runs a ferry from downtown to Logan airport across the bay that you probably also can't take. Since that was my destination for the morrow and I wanted to avoid the circuitous and likely confusing route bikes must use, I tried to call them after finding the number in a brochure at the Hostel. Apparently, passes are required there too. All I could get was a series of instructions that maddeningly send you toning all the phone buttons while eating

58

up three of my "kwarters." I finally got a message that the information number is closed until tomorrow morning and that I could leave a message. I did just that. Nastydavid.

Our final day was one of parting and finding our respective ways to transportation "out of there." I am sure there are people who have fun visiting Boston. I'm just not one of them, at least while biking. Tom and I found breakfast in a Greek restaurant near the Hostel and rode to a separation point where I could cross to Cambridge and he could turn south for the AMTRAK station. I watched him depart down a street which I could tell led to a construction area and a dead end. He was by then too far to yell to, so I watched as he turned around, returned to the corner, and angled down the one heading the right direction. Took one last picture of him and watched till he was gone. I was sad and also hopeful that he wouldn't get lost in the madhouse and honking Boston traffic. I then crossed the bridge over the Charles River and found my 20- mile long-way ride to the airport, getting only slightly lost. The sun was out and I could navigate celestially knowing the direction I wanted. The flight home was less dramatic than the labor-disputed Northwest Airlines flight to Seattle two months earlier. I reminisced about our ride, thought of Tom sitting on that train for three nights, and "what's next?" Don't know if I would do *this* trip again but knew I would long for another "big" trip.

CYCLISTS MAKE IT!
GRUMPY OLD BIKERS FINISH 5500
MILE CROSS COUNTRY TRIP IN BOOTHBAY

Postscript

Tom O'Brien skipped Cycle Oregon 1998 to protest the cost. He continued to ride, however, accumulating over 10,000 miles for the year, easily beating his previous record year of 7,661. He also reported that he lost 15 pounds (from a body that wasn't that big to begin with). He concluded that we must have had the best weather of any cross-country riders in '98 and attributed that mostly to our strategy of sitting out storms. He met other bikers on the AMTRAK back to Portland. The tandem couple we had been chasing at the end of our tour turned out to be Wayne and Penny from Carson City, Nevada and not the Sacramento couple we had left in Curlew, Washington. They were also pulling a Bob trailer. Tom found out from them that the gravel road west of Glacier Park was okay riding. He also met Bonnie from Eugene, Oregon who had ridden the GTE Big Ride. Tom says she described it as "hell with rain, hail, snow, and bitter cold weather, almost every big city that was possible, numerous accidents, and sometimes no food for the last ones in."(Like Roger Carlson from Maine, she wouldn't likely do it again.)

Scott, Sarah, and Lisa made it to Quoddy Head State Park near Lubec, Maine. This is well northeast of Bar Harbor and as far east as it is possible to go in the U.S.A. (except Puerto Rico?). Scott said they wished the U.S.A. stretched all the way to England so they could keep riding. He described meeting other bikers around the Great Lakes including a robust retired couple (presumably the Thomases) and a missionary who was on his 12th or 13th crossing. Their route was: across Michigan's Upper Peninsula (the "UP"), Sault Ste. Marie, part of the Trans-Canada (Highway 17) to Manitoulin Island, the ferry to the Bruce Peninsula (between Lakes George and Huron), Niagara Falls, and on to New England. They arrived in Boston August 24th (seven days after Tom & I) and had 4,787 miles.

Jason also made it to Quoddy Head. He was within a day or two of Scott and the girls, as they all found out later. How long they stayed together after Winnipeg wasn't in any of their letters. He also went across the UP to Sault Ste. Marie and rode the Trans-Canada. He described the Trans-Canada as very bad and "bumming him out over the road, the cars, the hills and the people." He met a girl there and started "free camping" which I assume is pulling over along the side of the road and camping as out-of-sight as possible. He apparently did not do the Manitoulin Island/Bruce Peninsula route as he reported stopping in Ottawa before dropping down into New York State. In Vermont, Jason met a Fife and Drum Corps group which "adopted" him and let him participate in their activities and parades. He did Kancamagus Pass in New Hampshire's White Mountains as did Tom and I, but, unlike our uneventful ride, he saw moose and bear. After Quoddy Head, he biked to Bangor where he caught a bus for Michigan and home. He described the trip as "the best time of his life." He is back to working in the bike shop, riding lots of single track, and planning to attend a frame-building course in Ashland, Oregon.

Dave and Julia DeCamp ran into the same rainstorm we had after Grand Forks, North Dakota, and then reported that they then had *no bad weather all the rest of the way to Vermont.* They met two bikers from Boston in Floodwood, MN and rode with them for 10 days. Like Scott, they did the UP, Manitoulin Island, the Bruce Peninsula and Niagara Falls. Like Jason, they did not like the stretch of the Trans-Canada and reported they "were scared for their lives." New York State was "bikers paradise" and they arrived in Vermont two weeks before Tom and me. They described their wedding as "perfect."

I made it home to join the Boethlings' southern Minnesota tour. The weather for that was as bad as it had been in July, with either wilting heat and humidity or rain. I continued to ride between jobs for clients and did a two-week tour of Tuscany, Italy, in October with my wife, Dana, and five other bicyclists from the Arrowheads bike team. Like Tom, I also had a record year, making over 12,000 miles for the first time.

May the wind be on your back, unless it's too hot for that.

Appendix - The Trip

Day	Destination	Overnight	Mileages, Tom	Dave
6-11	Seattle,WA	YH	11	27
6-12	Anacortes, WA	camped	87	100
6-13	Marblemount, WA	camped	91	100
6-14	Mazama, WA	camped	83	100
6-15	Riverside, WA	camped	67	67
6-16	Curlew, WA	camped	77	101
6-17	Ione, WA	motel	94	96
6-18	Sandpoint, ID	camped	90	101
6-19	Troy, MT	camped	93	102
6-20	Eureka, MT	camped	94	101
6-21	Avalanche Lake, MT	camped	98	112
6-22	Babb, MT	camped	3	43
6-23	Cut Bank, MT	camped	104	107
6-24	Hingham, MT	camped	100	100
6-25	Harlem, MT	camped	79	80
6-26	Malta, MT	motel	51	50
6-27	Malta, MT	motel	0	0
6-28	Wolf Point, MT	camped	126	124
6-29	Williston, ND	camped	104	106
6-30	New Town, ND	camped	78	84
7-1	Surrey, ND	camped	88	101
7-2	Rugby, ND	camped	72	71
7-3	Devils Lake, ND	camped	74	73
7-4	Grand Forks, ND	motel	104	105
7-5	Warren, MN	motel	37	35
7-6	Lake Bronson, MN	camped	58	64
7-7	St. Malo, Manitoba	camped	61	60
7-8	Winnipeg, Manitoba	camped	60	65
7-9	Birds Hill, Manitoba	camped	33	27
7-10	Birds Hill, Manitoba	camped	5	6
7-11	Birds Hill, Manitoba	camped	37	37
7-12	Birds Hill, Manitoba	camped	0	0
7-13	Oklee, MN	house	73	73
7-14	Itasca Park, MN	YH	72	71
7-15	Breezy Point, MN	camped	97	101
7-16	Mora, MN	house	100	105

Appendix - The Trip, continued

Day	Destination	Overnight	Mileage, Tom	Dave
7-17	Minneapolis, MN	house	83	83
7-18	Minneapolis, MN	house	29	43
7-19	Minneapolis, MN	house	0	32
7-20	Waterville, MN	camped	90	100
7-21	Clear Lake, IA	camped	105	105
7-22	Eldora, IA	camped	83	83
7-23	Cedar Falls, IA	camped	60	72
7-24	Monticello, IA	camped	100	100
7-25	Clinton IA	house	97	100
7-26	Bradford, IL	camped	89	90
7-27	Odell, IL	camped	84	101
7-28	Rensselaer, IN	camped	110	109
7-29	Salamonie River, IN	camped	109	110
7-30	Paulding, OH	camped	83	85
7-31	Pemberville, OH	camped	94	103
8-1	Belden, OH	camped	92	101
8-2	Willoughby, OH	house	72	73
8-3	Cambridge Spr., PA	camped	100	100
8-4	Onoville, NY	camped	90	101
8-5	Letchworth Park, NY	camped	101	103
8-6	Wolcott, NY	camped	103	104
8-7	Pulaski, NY	camped	61	62
8-8	Inlet, NY	camped	100	101
8-9	Ticonderoga, NY	camped	105	105
8-10	Sharon, VT	motel	81	103
8-11	N. Woodstock, NH	camped	76	80
8-12	Conway, NH	YH	42	48
8-13	Boothbay, ME	camped	118	118
8-14	Boothbay, ME	camped	46	48
8-15	Kennebunkport, ME	camped	90	100
8-16	Salisbury, MA	camped	76	78
8-17	Boston, MA	YH	55	56
8-18	Airport/AMTRAK	-	4	15
Totals			5,169	5,505